Forster's Women:
Eternal Differences

Forster's Women: Eternal Differences

Bonnie Blumenthal Finkelstein

COLUMBIA UNIVERSITY PRESS
NEW YORK AND LONDON 1975

The Andrew W. Mellon Foundation, through a special grant, has assisted the Press in publishing this volume.

Bonnie Blumenthal Finkelstein is currently assistant professor of English at Montgomery County Community College in Blue Bell, Pennsylvania.

Library of Congress Cataloging in Publication Data

Finkelstein, Bonnie Blumenthal.
    Forster's women: eternal differences.

    Bibliography: p. 173
    1. Forster, Edward Morgan, 1879–1970—Characters—Women. I. Title.
PR6011.O58Z654   823'.9'12   74-18418
ISBN 0-231-03893-3

To Richard and my Parents

Preface

E. M. Forster's novels portray the struggle of individuals to be unique. They take place in a social world in which both men and women are oppressed by arbitrary sex roles and stereotypes; dogmatic convention is the villain in all his works. Forster's conventional society demands that its full participants be male, heterosexual, and athletic, and all his protagonists lack at least one of those traits. They are, therefore, different. Often similar to each other only in that differentness, women and homosexuals share many of the same problems, since both are thwarted by a society which would deny them acceptance as real people. Forster's protagonists are all outsiders, who must in the course of their novels accept their differentness and learn to follow Margaret Schlegel's advice to her sister in *Howards End:*

It is only that people are far more different than is pretended. All over the world men and women are worrying because they cannot develop as they are supposed to develop. . . . Develop what you have. . . . It is a part of the battle against sameness. Differences—eternal differences, planted by God in a single family, so that there may always be colour; sorrow perhaps, but colour in the daily grey.

Forster's greatest characters are women, and his novels closely examine the problems of women in society; but his overall theme is a larger one in which women function as representatives of all humanity.[1] This androgynous ideal[2] in Forster's works is not a leveling one; it does not seek to eradicate differences between people but to heighten them. It insists that the only eternal differences are individual rather than arbitrary, and here Forster departs from the conventional, sexually polarized Victorian soci-

1. Previous criticism on Forster, while valuable, does not view women in quite this way.
2. For a thorough discussion of the tradition of the androgynous ideal, see Carolyn G. Heilbrun, *Toward a Recognition of Androgyny* (New York, Knopf, 1973).

ety in which he grew up. Here Forster most clearly shows the love
of uniqueness that characterized the rebellious Bloomsbury group
to which he belonged.

Bloomsbury believed that each individual human being possesses a full range of human potential; that each person must
strive, not to be manly or ladylike, but to be human. Bloomsbury's
spirit was androgynous and held personal relations to be the highest good: relations between persons who were equal yet unique,
regardless of gender. Friendship and passion were equally approved, and both sexual and platonic relations were accepted between men, between man and woman, and between women.
Bloomsbury's open acceptance of sexuality as positive, together
with the bisexuality of most of the members of the group, sheds
much light on Forster's ideas of sexuality in general and homosexuality in particular. The keynote is tolerance, variety, and respect
for reasoned individual judgment.

Bloomsbury believed in the value of individual attempts to lead
a good moral life. This, with Forster's belief in life's complexity
and in nonpolarized sex roles, gives him a nonpolarized view of
the world: he rejects imperialism and class snobbery, and he
shares with Bloomsbury a faith in the importance of self-
knowledge as a prelude to that good moral life.

Yet Forster cannot be fully defined by the epithet "Bloomsbury," any more than any person can be fully defined by the
labels "male," "female," or "homosexual." He remains unique,
eternally different; and his humanist, androgynous vision remains
radical fifty years after he wrote his last novel.

I would like to thank the following publishers for permission to
quote extensively from the works of E. M. Forster: Alfred A.
Knopf, Inc., for permission to quote from *Where Angels Fear to
Tread, The Longest Journey, A Room with a View,* and *Howards End;*
Harcourt Brace Jovanovich, Inc., for permission to quote from *A
Passage to India;* W. W. Norton and Company, Inc. for permission to
quote from *Maurice;* and the British publisher of all six novels,
Edward Arnold (Publishers) Ltd. I would like especially to mention
the kindness of W. W. Norton and Company, Inc., who sent me early
proofs of *Maurice* several months before its publication so that I
could spend the summer of 1971 working on the dissertation that
formed the basis for this book. I would also like to thank New
Directions Publishing Corporation for permission to quote from
Lionel Trilling's *E. M. Forster.*

I would like to thank Jane Ashcom (formerly Jane Balsham), whose excellent teaching first directed my interests into literature; Robert Bamberg, who at the University of Pennsylvania further directed me to the modern novel; the late Herbert Howarth, who first exposed me to Forster; Lionel Trilling, whose brilliant book on Forster was indispensable and who spent time at Columbia giving me enormously helpful background information on Forster's life; Daniel Dodson, whose unfailing eye for typos is inhuman and whose knowledge of Italy kept chapters 1 and 3 honest; Carolyn Heilbrun, my mentor, who more than anyone else is the intellectual progenitor of this book and who gave me invaluable advice as it grew, whose good humor and wise good sense kept me going through the whole ordeal; my parents, who encouraged me in my desire to be a teacher and a scholar from the time that I first announced that to be my ambition, when I was fourteen, and whose moral and financial support made it happen; and especially Richard, who lived through it all with me, and who has never felt "that he must lead women, though he knew not whither, and protect them, though he knew not against what."

Contents

Forster's Women:
Eternal Differences

One
Where Angels Fear to Tread

Forster's concern with sexual stereotypes is evident from his first published novel, *Where Angels Fear to Tread*. In this book he creates four characters who brilliantly illustrate the problems of women: Mrs. Herriton, the Woman as Manipulator who sees all of life, especially family life, as a game of power politics; Lilia Theobald Herriton Carella, the flighty beauty who never bothers to develop her brains and who suffers as Woman Imprisoned by Marriage; Harriet Herriton, the narrow, conventional spinster who seeks salvation in religious fanaticism; and Caroline Abbott, the sensitive, intelligent woman who tries to avoid the fates of the others. The novel follows Caroline's development into an aware, mature human being whom we are able to consider a person as well as a woman, for she is the only one who seeks to understand and then transcend society's accepted roles for women. She is neither mother, sister, nor wife; she cannot be defined only in relation to a man. She learns to accept her own sexuality, but fulfillment is impossible because, in the world of this novel, the brotherhood of man is effected at the expense of the sisterhood and even freedom of women. Her fate is not a happy one. To understand why, we must first examine the women whom she does not seek to emulate.

In evaluating the emptiness and meaninglessness of his mother's life, Philip Herriton deals with three different attempts by women to lead full and useful lives—all failures.

But he sets up a hierarchy for their failures: he considers Lilia "with her clutches after pleasure" and Harriet "with her gloomy peevish creed" to be "more divine" than his mother, a "well-ordered, active, useless machine." [1] Mrs. Herriton's failure is the most depressing and the most frightening, for she is a capable, vital person, a success by the standards of her own village of Sawston, the ideal woman who has internalized society's definition of her role and has emerged useless and manipulative. Because Harriet and Lilia are individually flawed and unattractive, their failures are less representative and therefore less awful. If taken together, however, each can represent the extreme of one of society's definitions of roles for women: Harriet, religious and pure, as the Blessed Virgin Mary, and Lilia, a flighty sex object, as Eve. When combined still further, with Mrs. Herriton as mother, these three women fairly well cover all the options open to women. The failure of Mrs. Herriton remains the most upsetting because she is the most potentially attractive character.

Mrs. Herriton believes in domestic life to the exclusion of all else; she does not believe "in romance nor in transfiguration, nor in parallels from history, nor in anything else that may disturb domestic life" (*A,* p. 8). Significantly, she has no first name, and is defined only by her role as a wife and by her husband's name. Forster withholds first names from two groups of his characters: (1) those men and women to whom he wishes to impute an impersonal kind of wisdom (Mr. Emerson of *A Room with a View,* Miss Avery of *Howards End,* [2] and Mrs. Moore of *A Passage to India*); and

1. E. M. Forster, *Where Angels Fear to Tread* (New York, Vintage paperback, 1958), p. 87. All references to this work will follow the pagination of this readily available edition and will appear in the text in the abbreviated form *A.*
2. Ruth Wilcox, who also possesses impersonal wisdom in *Howards End,* is given a first name probably to avoid confusion with Margaret Schlegel, who becomes the second Mrs. Wilcox. Lionel Trilling, *E. M. Forster* (Norfolk, Conn., New Directions, 1943), p. 119, suggests, "It is perhaps significant that her name is Ruth, for her heart is sad, the home for which she is sick is her chief passion, and she stands amid alien corn."

(2) those women whom he wishes to represent as defined solely by their roles as wives and mothers (Mrs. Herriton of *Where Angels Fear to Tread,* Mrs. Elliot of *The Longest Journey,* and Mrs. Hall and Mrs. Durham of *Maurice*).

Mrs. Herriton's most outstanding negative characteristics, "her diplomacy, her insincerity, her continued repression of vigour," are purposeless, making no one any better or happier, not even herself (*A,* p. 87). Her most outstanding positive characteristic, her vitality, her "gift of making work a treat" (*A,* p. 13), has no effective creative outlet. Her gardening, which at first connects her in our minds with Mrs. Wilcox, is denied fruit precisely because of her overriding concern for manipulation and power politics: when she receives word of Lilia's engagement to Gino from Mrs. Theobald, she is so furious at not being told directly that she forgets to cover up the peas she is sowing in neat, orderly rows, the best she has ever sown (*A,* p. 14). Terribly insulted that Lilia should dare to live her own life without consulting her, she remembers the peas too late: "The sparrows had taken every one. But countless fragments of the letter remained, disfiguring the tidy ground" (*A,* p. 20).

In *Howards End,* love of and ability at work are primary virtues in the Wilcox men, and Margaret Schlegel hopes that the time will come when all women, as well as all men, will work as a matter of course.[3] But in Mrs. Herriton's world this time has not yet come; women are not allowed by convention to do any real work. They must find other outlets for their energies, and Mrs. Herriton directs hers into trying to live through her children and run their lives:

It was now nearly ten years since Charles had fallen in love with Lilia Theobald because she was pretty, and during that time Mrs. Herriton had hardly known a moment's rest. For six months she schemed to prevent the match, and when it had taken place she

3. E. M. Forster, *Howards End* (New York, Vintage paperback, 1954), p. 110. All future references to this work will follow the pagination of this readily available edition and will appear in the body of the text in the abbreviated form *HE.*

turned to another task—the supervision of her daughter-in-law. Lilia must be pushed through life without bringing discredit on the family into which she had married.

[*A,* pp. 8–9]

Even after Charles dies, Mrs. Herriton continues to try to conventionalize and to tame Lilia, to teach her "the duties of widowhood and motherhood" (*A,* p. 10). Mrs. Herriton excels in the role of spokeswoman for and defender of the "proper" role for women. But the irony is obvious: if one succeeds in being proper, one becomes Mrs. Herriton, clearly a ghastly end. And the dilemma does not stop here. Mrs. Herriton does not have imagination but "intuition, a more useful quality, and the picture she made to herself of Lilia's *fiancé* did not prove altogether wrong" (*A,* p. 19).

Mrs. Herriton is concerned primarily with appearances and embodies what Caroline comes to recognize as "petty unselfishness" (*A,* p. 76): "She could not bear to seem less charitable than others" (*A,* p. 87). Chronically insincere, she occasionally loses control and her real feelings surface, providing her with a rare emotional outlet that only serves to underscore how bottled up she generally is. When Caroline refuses to take Gino's rejection of Sawston's offer of aid as final, Mrs. Herriton explodes, and Philip is shocked: "This outburst of violence from his elegant ladylike mother pained him dreadfully. He had not known that it was in her" (*A,* p. 91).

Mrs. Herriton always looks for an ulterior motive beneath surface intentions and communicates that approach to life to her son Philip. When we read that she "always asked her children's advice where possible" (*A,* p. 70), we assume that she is a considerate mother who treats her children as individuals and respects their opinions; but we soon see that this is merely another form of manipulation. She elicits the desired response from Philip when she wonders what Gino's motive can be for sending Lilia's daughter, Irma, postcards from her baby brother: "Two years before, Philip would have said that the motive was to give pleasure. Now he, like his mother, tried to think of something sinister and subtle" (*A,* p. 81).

Manipulation is portrayed as an essentially feminine trait, *the* most important feminine device for personal communication. The first glimpse we have of Lilia shows her "playing" Mr. Kingcroft, as Philip notes (*A,* p. 7). But she is not the most egregious example; Mrs. Herriton surely deserves that title, with Harriet merely doing her bidding and Caroline attempting to out-manipulate the master. Sawston is a world run by women, and Philip sees himself as being worked on by three forces, all female. When he sees Caroline in the hotel, he snaps; "To be run by his mother and hectored by his sister was as much as he could stand. The intervention of a third female drove him suddenly beyond politeness" (*A,* p. 102). Caroline alone of all the women in the book recognizes and apologizes for her lapses into manipulation. She admits trying to run Philip as his mother does (*A,* p. 153), but Philip has become, perhaps because of his mother, the sort of detached observer who almost demands such a response. This does not exonerate Caroline, but merely explains her. Forster implies the existence of a vicious cycle: a manipulative mother creates a weak, dependent son who in turn evokes manipulative responses from his female contemporaries. Obviously, this cycle must be broken somewhere; Caroline represents the only hope for the future in this book, for Philip is too totally in his mother's power to rebel, and Mrs. Herriton can conceive of no other form of behavior.

Mrs. Herriton tolerates Philip's whims in order to get what she wants. She is aware of what she is doing, and articulates her strategy to Harriet in "the memorable words, 'Let Philip say what he likes, and he will let us do what we like'" (*A,* p. 14). Eventually Philip also becomes aware of her calculated manipulation of him:

He was sure that she was not impulsive, but did not dare to say so. Her ability frightened him. All his life he had been her puppet. She let him worship Italy, and reform Sawston—just as she had let Harriet be Low Church. She had let him talk as much as he liked. But when she wanted a thing she always got it.

[*A*, p. 86]

This is reminiscent of the end of *Man and Superman*, where Ann, who is Everywoman, magnanimously allows Tanner to "Go on talking." [4]

Mrs. Herriton's manipulation is all indirect. When she is upset because Caroline is going to Italy to get the baby, her first reaction is to send Philip. Her second reaction is to send Harriet, too. It never occurs to her to go herself, for indirection is an integral part of her approach to life. Women are not allowed to do most things directly: Mrs. Herriton does nothing directly. The whole affair is totally hypocritical on her part; she doesn't care at all about the child. It is considered proper for women, especially mothers, to use other people, especially their children, to effect what they want, and Mrs. Herriton is nothing if not proper. She considers her daughter a failure because she lacks the flexibility and deviousness which are necessary to manipulate others: "Though pious and patriotic, and a great moral asset for the house, she lacked that pliancy and tact which her mother so much valued, and had expected her to pick up for herself" (*A*, p. 13). Harriet herself does not manipulate, but she agrees to the manipulation and goes to Italy to see that Philip does his duty as a puppet, which upsets him considerably (*A*, p. 96). Philip's only source of self-respect is his amused-observer status, his understanding of what is going on: "Harriet, worked by her mother; Mrs. Herriton, worked by Miss Abbott; Gino, worked by a cheque—what better entertainment could he desire? . . . He might be a

4. George Bernard Shaw, *Man and Superman* (Baltimore, Maryland, Penguin, 1962), p. 212. All references to this work will follow the pagination of this readily available edition.

puppet's puppet, but he knew exactly the disposition of the strings" (*A*, p. 94).

Toward the end of the novel, Philip tells Gino that "This affair *is* being managed by the ladies." Gino's response is crucial; when he laughs "Ah, the ladies—the ladies!" (*A*, p. 154), we see for the first time the attitude of conventional male society, the tolerant acceptance of the games of inferior beings that perpetuates manipulation as women's only weapon. Clearly, manipulation by women will be accepted by men as long as the men have the real power, to the detriment of both sexes.

Mrs. Herriton sees family life as an exercise in power politics, a sort of "domestic imperialism," [5] but she tries to avoid admitting that this is her approach. She strongly objects to Philip's use of the word "tactics" in reference to their plans for the baby and prefers the more neutral word "course" instead (*A*, p. 72).

The relationship based on domestic imperialism, so well depicted between Philip and his mother, is reflected in the marriage between Lilia and Gino. Lilia is twelve years older than Gino and in many ways attempts to use him as Mrs. Herriton uses Philip. She always treats Gino "as a boy, which he was, and as a fool, which he was not, thinking herself so immeasurably superior to him that she neglected opportunity after opportunity of establishing her rule" (*A*, p. 43). Even Caroline Abbott refers to Lilia's "managing" Gino, or more precisely to her failure to do so: "Lilia . . . must have been cowardly. He was only a boy—just going to turn into something fine, I thought—and she must have mismanaged him" (*A*, p. 77). Gino also sees marriage in this way and asserts that "there should be one master in that house—himself" (*A*, p. 42).

The extent to which Mrs. Herriton views family life as a game of power politics can be seen most clearly in her deal-

5. Alan Mintz, "Varieties of Homosexual Society and the Early Novels of Forster" (unpublished essay, 1969), p. 16.

ings with Mrs. Theobald and Irma, Lilia's mother and daughter. Mrs. Herriton considers Mrs. Theobald a threat to her own power over Irma and is glad that she falls ill: "fortunately old Mrs. Theobald, who had attempted interference, began to break up" (*A*, p. 9). Forster's irony is impressive when he describes Mrs. Herriton's reaction to Lilia's attempt at filial devotion: "Charles died, and the struggle recommenced. Lilia tried to assert herself, and said that she should go to take care of Mrs. Theobald. It required all Mrs. Herriton's kindness to prevent her" (*A*, p. 9). After Lilia's marriage to Gino, Mrs. Herriton forces Mrs. Theobald to choose sides (A, p. 20), and Mrs. Theobald, a weak person and no match for Mrs. Herriton, sides against her daughter (*A*, p. 57). However, when Mrs. Herriton attempts to use Mrs. Theobald again, as an excuse for her own inactivity with regard to the baby, Caroline objects and causes Mrs. Herriton to blush by asking, "does not Mrs. Theobald always take any initiative from you?" (*A*, p. 84).

Mrs. Herriton's relationship with Irma is somewhat less straightforward than that with Mrs. Theobald, for a relationship based on power between an adult and a child is not commonly considered to be as reprehensible as a similar one between two adults. At first Mrs. Herriton seems to be not a bad grandmother, affectionate if stuffy in her fond insistence on not being called "Granny" (*A*, p. 6). When we first see the two of them they are together at the train station as Lilia leaves for Italy with Mrs. Herriton's blessings, and Mrs. Herriton's first words in the novel are a promise that Irma will be good (*A*, p. 4). We soon see that she is trying to run Irma just as she had tried to run Lilia, to live vicariously through others:

She was getting proud of Irma, who had certainly greatly improved, and could no longer be called that most appalling of things—a vulgar child. She was anxious to form her before her mother returned.

[*A*, p. 11]

If we are appalled early at Mrs. Herriton's attempt to win Irma away from her mother's family (*A*, p. 9), we are even more appalled at her attempt to win Irma away from her mother. Lilia's Italian trip has been planned by the Herritons as a means of getting rid of her, of removing her influence from Irma (*A*, p. 7). Although Mrs. Herriton is presented as "a loyal supporter of parental authority" (*A*, p. 11) to whom a child's disobedience is the "eighth deadly sin, so convenient to parents and guardians" (*A*, p. 83), her theory of child-raising depends on a parental ideal, not on parental love. She therefore considers Lilia unfit to raise or even influence Irma:

All a child's life depends on the ideal it has of its parents. Destroy that and everything goes—morals, behaviour, everything. Absolute trust in some one else is the essence of education. This is why I have been so careful about talking of poor Lilia before her.

[*A*, p. 70]

Mrs. Herriton conceals Lilia's death from Irma and asserts that "she never cared for her mother" (*A*, p. 70) anyway, but she oversteps her power in attempting to conceal the existence of Irma's baby brother. Both inexcusable and ineffective, an attempt to suppress brotherhood can lead only to spiritual decay. In *The Longest Journey*, Agnes commits the same sin, inextricably linking her in our minds with Mrs. Herriton. Mrs. Herriton is also guilty of suppressing sisterhood, and here she is successful. Lilia, in an attempt to educate the next generation of women to the evils of marriage, wants Irma to have her diary, which traces "all the causes and the growth of her misery" (*A*, p. 66). Mrs. Herriton intercepts it and does not allow Irma to learn from her mother's fate; Mrs. Herriton has too great an emotional stake in the status quo to allow change.

Lilia, Mrs. Herriton's most pathetic victim, flees England, her mother-in-law's manipulation, and her own probable future as a manipulative matriarch only to find herself in an even worse position as an oppressed Italian wife. Manipulation and oppression, the only two options open to her, are unsatisfactory, and their failure points out the failure of the two existing systems to deal fairly with half their population. That Lilia is not an attractive character nor a particularly impressive person does not make her suffering any less moving. As a victim of society she is Everywoman, and, by extension, Everyperson.

When the novel opens, Lilia is the focal point; her departure for Italy brings everyone together and introduces them to us: "They were all at Charing Cross to see Lilia off— Philip, Harriet, Irma, Mrs. Herriton herself. Even Mrs. Theobald" (*A*, p. 3). The first thing we're told about Lilia is that she's giddy, that "the sight of so many people talking at once and saying such different things caused Lilia to break into ungovernable peals of laughter" (*A*, p. 3). The image for Lilia's escape from England is significant: "laughing helplessly, she was carried out into the fog" (*A*, p. 6). Lilia, giddy, helpless before her laughter, whose "one qualification for life was rather blowsy high spirits, which turned querulous or boisterous according to circumstances" (*A*, p. 57), is ironically presented as a chaperone for Caroline Abbott. But it is Lilia, not Caroline, who is in a fog, helpless, childlike, and passive—in short, "feminine" by society's standards. Only Lilia, however, thinks of herself as chaperone (*A*, p. 4); everyone else is very aware that in reality Caroline is chaperoning her (*A*, p. 7). The reasons for Lilia's needing a chaperone are complex and transcend her own personality: she is too successful as a feminine woman to be treated as an adult by others, even by other women, for they have developed their own options along different lines. Lilia cannot understand why the Herritons blame Caroline for her marriage to Gino (*A*, p. 35); she considers herself an adult, a person, and never fully realizes that no one else does the same. Like Lucy Honeychurch in *A Room with a View*, Lilia does not think that she needs a chaperone; also like Lucy,

Lilia balks at constantly being told what is and what is not proper, with what is proper always being in the direction of the constricting and the negative. That she is older than Lucy only makes her situation more pathetic: her character is too firmly developed along the lines of the feminine woman to allow her the escape into personhood that Lucy will achieve with George.

To understand why Lilia flees England we have only to look at her life at Sawston, where she exists only as "Mrs. Charles" (*A*, p. 5). After Charles's death, her role as widow is even more restrictive than her role as wife, and she is "continually subject to the refining influence of her late husband's family" (*A*, p. 9). She does not even choose her own house; one is "taken for her" (*A*, p. 9), and then she is criticized for not taking care of it properly: "She was a bad housekeeper, always in the throes of some domestic crisis, which Mrs. Herriton, who kept her servants for years, had to step across and adjust" (*A*, p. 10). Then, as now, keeping house was seen as woman's primary job, although supervising servants hardly seems a full-time, fulfilling occupation. Not surprisingly, Lilia seeks other outlets for her energies, but her every attempt is thwarted by the Herritons:

She learnt to bicycle, for the purpose of waking the place up, and coasted down the High Street one Sunday evening, falling off at the turn by the church. If she had not been a relative, it would have been entertaining. But even Philip, who in theory loved outraging English conventions, rose to the occasion and gave her a talking to which she remembered to her dying day.

[*A*, p. 10]

Lilia's approach to life is unconventional; she does not subscribe to Sawston's rigid intolerance of any emotion that is not institutionalized. Mrs. Herriton rebukes her for liking Mr. Kingcroft "extremely" but not being "exactly engaged" (*A*, p. 9) to him; to Mrs. Herriton, one is either engaged or one is not, "since no intermediate state existed" (*A*, p. 9).

This is a remarkable comment on the inflexibility of middle-class society: everything must be categorized properly or it is not allowed to exist. In *Howards End,* Mrs. Wilcox must answer a similar objection from Charles, who is amazed that she refers to Helen and Paul's love for one another, however brief, as an engagement (*HE,* p. 23). To Charles Wilcox, as to Mrs. Herriton and to Forster's philistines generally, it is the labels which count; to his sympathetic characters, it is the emotions themselves. When Lilia gives in and apologizes to Mrs. Herriton, we fear that she is capitulating; when she rejects England forever by marrying an Italian, we wish her success. But worse follows.

Ironically, Philip can accept Lilia as a human being only in Italy (*A,* p. 23), for, as Lilia discovers, Italy does not allow its own women that privilege. When she welcomes Philip to Monteriano, however, she has not yet discovered this; she looks radiant and very happy (*A,* p. 29). She seems not to expect Philip's negative reaction to her marriage and is infuriated into eloquence by his patronizing attitude toward her. She suddenly becomes articulate and for the first time reveals some intelligence. In answer to Philip's innuendo about Gino's family position (his father was a dentist), Lilia "adroitly picked out the only undesirable member of the Herriton clan" (*A,* p. 34). She declares herself a democrat as opposed to Philip, who is a snob, when she asserts, "for my own poor part, I think what people are is what matters, but I don't suppose you'll agree" (*A,* p. 34). She wounds Philip by describing one of Gino's cousins as "a lawyer just like you are—except that he has lots to do and can never get away" (*A,* p. 34). But her finest moment comes when Philip, who is indeed right in calling Gino a bully, offends all women by announcing that Gino will release her "when he sees he has a man to deal with" (*A,* p. 35). Lilia turns on "her gallant defender" and explodes into insight:

For once in my life I'll thank you to leave me alone. I'll thank your mother too. For twelve years you've trained me and tortured

me, and I'll stand it no more. Do you think I'm a fool? Do you
think I've never felt? Ah! when I came to your house a poor
young bride, how you all looked me over—never a kind word—
and discussed me, and thought I might just do; and your mother
corrected me, and your sister snubbed me, and you said funny
things about me to show how clever you were! And when Charles
died I was still to run in strings for the honour of your beastly
family, and I was to be cooped up at Sawston and learn to keep
house, and all my chances spoilt of marrying again. No, thank
you! No, thank you! "Bully?" "Insolent boy?" Who's that, pray,
but you? But, thank goodness, I can stand up against the world
now, for I've found Gino, and this time I'll marry for love!

[*A,* pp. 35–36]

Lilia's charges are all true; and Philip realizes it, opening
the door to his development into a better person. But there
are two great flaws in her argument. First, Italian life is no
solution; if anything, it's worse for women than Sawston.
Caroline Abbott, not Lilia, learns most from Lilia's fate and
recognizes and seeks personally to avoid Lilia's second great
error, the identification of sexual attraction alone with
"love." Lilia hardly knows Gino; the attraction is clearly sexual, but she sees it as love. Near the end of the book, Caroline sees her own attraction to Gino for what it is and is
therefore better able to cope with it; and she is also able to
benefit from the knowledge she has gained through Lilia's
experience of an Italian marriage.

Significantly, there is no verbal communication between
Lilia and Gino: she speaks no Italian, he no English (*A,* p.
31). Forster here stresses not only the deep differences between those two cultures, but also the lack of any real communication between men and women, husbands and wives.
Lilia and Gino seem to communicate better at the beginning
of their relationship, when still separated by language, than
they do later after language has ceased to be a difficulty.

When Lilia realizes that her marriage is a failure, she
becomes "as unhappy as it was possible for her nature to
be" (*A,* p. 55). She becomes possessive, which Gino resents

(*A*, p. 53)—a common situation with men whose wives have nothing to do and nowhere to go. "She had no unkind treatment, and few unkind words, from her husband. He simply left her alone" (*A*, p. 55). Because she is alone so much she loses the self-confidence which had dazzled Philip, and she becomes reflective in spite of herself and against her nature (*A*, p. 56). Thinking primarily about her marriage, Lilia "reflects" the way a mirror does and shows us what the state of marriage is like.

Gino, a man, succeeds where Mrs. Herriton, a woman, fails, in dominating Lilia: "in the most gentle way, which Mrs. Herriton might have envied, Gino made her do what he wanted" (*A*, p. 57). Lilia is frightened at Gino's brutality: when she asks for a tiny bit of freedom, to go for a walk alone, he forbids her; when she threatens to cut off his money, he terrifies her into submission (*A*, pp. 58–59). Gino asserts his "manhood" by keeping his women in line, and when Lilia and Perfetta cross themselves after Gino's outburst, Forster comments: "Thus did the two women pay homage to their outraged male" (*A*, p. 59). Lilia realizes that he married her for her money, but her realization does no good; "he had tamed her, and she never threatened to cut off supplies again" (*A*, p. 59).

Her last remnant of happiness disappears when she discovers Gino's infidelity; she "broke down utterly and sobbed" (*A*, p. 60). She feels terribly alone and has no options left:

She had given up everything for him—her daughter, her relatives, her friends, all the little comforts and luxuries of a civilized life—and even if she had the courage to break away, there was no one who would receive her now.

[*A*, p. 60]

At first she is afraid to accuse him and decides that it is "better to live on humbly, trying not to feel, endeavouring by a cheerful demeanour to put things right (*A*, p. 61). Totally cowed, she accepts whatever Gino does. "He was particularly kind to her when he hardly ever saw her, and she accepted his kindness without resentment, even with gratitude, so docile had she become" (*A*, p. 61). Her suffering is that of Everywoman:

Lilia had achieved pathos despite herself, for there are some situations in which vulgarity counts no longer. Not Cordelia nor Imogen more deserves our tears. . . . the wisest of women could hardly have suffered more.

[*A*, p. 61]

She asserts her freedom by going for a solitary evening walk, but returns to her "captivity" (*A*, p. 64) where she is accused by Gino and finally realizes that he is a "cruel, worthless, hypocritical, dissolute upstart" (*A*, p. 64). She accuses him of infidelity and is shocked by his reaction: he laughs at her. She never forgives him that laugh; the double standard is clearly not funny. But Lilia dies giving birth to the son Gino wants so much. Lilia, as woman, is necessary only long enough to fulfill her function of producing a male child. In the end we hardly know which oppression of Lilia's life is the worst, Italy's or Sawston's. Awful as her Italian life is, however, it is ultimately Sawston that destroys the only posterity she has: Harriet is responsible for the death of her son, Mrs. Herriton for the ignorance of her daughter. That Irma never reads her mother's diary and never learns of her mother's fate may quite possibly doom the child to repeating it.

Any attempt to understand Lilia's character must deal with the effect that beauty may have on a woman's development. Lilia's beauty allows her to remain shallow and superficial because nothing more is demanded of her. Charles falls in love with her specifically because she is pretty, and Gino's attraction to her, to the extent that it is not mercenary, is physical: he had "always desired a blonde" (*A*, p. 50). In *Howards End,* the fact that Margaret is not as pretty as

Helen in some way accounts for her superior sensitivity. And Adela Quested's lack of beauty contributes to her ability to achieve self-understanding and to act heroically—to be, in fact, a hero, as distinct from a heroine. Carolyn Heilbrun defines the "woman as hero" as "a woman who is the protagonist of a work, the character who undergoes the central action, the character whom men, as well as women, may view as an actor in a destiny possible for them" as opposed to a heroine, "that female character who plays the largest or most important role in the life of the hero." [6] Of all Forster's female heroes, only Lucy Honeychurch is pretty, and she is primarily a heroine, a passive character who is fortunate enough to be acted upon by the right person.

Society discusses female beauty, or the lack of it, more than male beauty, and Forster is no exception, although his interest in male beauty does lead him to use it symbolically (for example, the naked George Emerson in *A Room with a View* or the near-naked man who pulls the punkah in the courtroom in *A Passage to India*). Physical beauty is less crippling for Forster's men than for his women because the men are not allowed to let it define them totally; they must *do* something, too. Only Gerald and to some extent Aziz are negatively affected by their physical attractiveness; both possess a brutalized sexual snobbery that considers women, beautiful or not, to be inferior. On the other hand, Stephen Wonham, Maurice, and Alec are handsome and not brutalized. In *The Longest Journey,* most of the sympathetic male characters are ugly and take this as a sign of their salvation; the manipulative Agnes, however, is handsome.

Lilia's inability to plumb the depths of Gino's character (*A,* p. 43) relates to her beauty, and the consequent fact that she never had to develop any depths of her own. She is barely an adult; in fact, she talks baby-talk in public, to

6. Carolyn Heilbrun, "The Woman as Hero," *Texas Quarterly,* 8 (Winter 1965), 132–33.

Philip (*A*, p. 30). A child-woman, Lilia has never developed any sense of adult responsibilities. Women in general are kept from maturing in their own cultures: Caroline can only mature in Italy, by learning from Lilia's experience, and Caroline is not pretty.

If women are not encouraged to grow up in England, they are not encouraged to exist in Italy, as Lilia discovers. Out of her element in a strange foreign world (*A*, p. 56), a man's world, as Italy is outside the home, Lilia functions as symbol for all women, out of their element in a world ruled by and for men. Lilia is Everywoman; Italy is Everywhere, "such a delightful place to live in if you happen to be a man. . . . the brotherhood of man is a reality. But it is accomplished at the expense of the sisterhood of women" (*A*, p. 47).

Women are totally insulated from male friendship:

Why should you not make friends with your neighbour at the theatre or in the train, when you know and he knows that feminine criticism and feminine insight and feminine prejudice will never come between you? Though you become as David and Jonathan, you need never enter his home, nor he yours.

[*A*, p. 47]

The reference to David and Jonathan is possibly homosexual, foreshadowing *Maurice*. As we see in *Maurice*, homosexuals, like women, are severely oppressed by society; yet they do benefit from all the advantages described here, all the privileges available to men because of their superior position in society.

The role of women in Italian life is incredibly oppressive; by denying male friendship to its women, Italy essentially denies them any friendship:

Meanwhile, the women—they have, of course, their house and their church, with its admirable and frequent services, to which they are escorted by the maid. Otherwise they do not go out

much, for it is not genteel to walk, and you are too poor to keep a
carriage.

[*A*, p. 47]

Gino keeps Lilia isolated, according to Italian custom. She is
not fulfilled by either of her two options, her house or the
church. Her house, bought because she thought it suited
Gino and because she wanted her house and her man
together, is not enough, if only because Gino will not stay in
it with her. The church is equally unsatisfactory; Lilia, not
being Catholic (although she does nominally convert), is effectively cut off from the traditional Italian female occupation. However, being cut off from Santa Deodata is a good
thing.

Santa Deodata is Passive Woman to an absurd degree: "all
her life she lay upon her back . . . refusing to eat, refusing
to play, refusing to work" (*A*, p. 100). Forster delightfully
says of a girl who does absolutely nothing that she "was only
fifteen when she died, which shows how much is within the
reach of any schoolgirl" (*A*, p. 100). Santa Deodata's story,
unlike Lilia's, is funny: "It is a gentle saint who is content
with half another saint to see her die. In her death, as in
her life, Santa Deodata did not accomplish much" (*A*, p.
149). Yet however absurd, the medieval Italian religious
woman is more bearable than the modern English one; to
Philip, "Santa Deodata was better company than Harriet"
(*A*, p. 101). In England, at least, religion is no longer generally accepted as valuable, as it was in the Middle Ages, and
the role of women as religious mainstay is no longer as important. The women involved therefore seem rather irrele-
vant. Another more ironic and personal explanation relates to another part of the Santa Deodata story: when her
mother was thrown down the stairs, "so holy was the saint
that she never picked her mother up, but lay upon her back
through all, and thus assured her throne in Paradise" (*A*, p.

100). Just possibly, Philip would like to lie watching while his mother suffered a similar fate.

Although Gino is hardly ever home, he nevertheless considers himself unequivocally "master" (*A,* p. 42). At first he doesn't interfere with Lilia because she is older, richer, and English; but soon all this is canceled out by the fact that she is "woman":

he realized for the first time the responsibilities of married life. He must save her from dangers, physical and social, for after all she was a woman. "And I," he reflected, "though I am young, am at all events a man, and know what is right."

[*A,* p. 48]

In Italy wives are dehumanized; Gino's friend agrees that he should keep Lilia isolated, since "The more precious a possession the more carefully it should be guarded" (*A,* p. 55). Women are equated with objects, to be locked in stifling rooms where no one comes and no one is allowed out. The double standard applied to social life applies to sexual life as well; Gino thinks it perfectly acceptable for him to have an affair but does not extend that right to Lilia (*A,* p. 60). In fact, when Gino laughs at Lilia's accusation of infidelity, his cousin Perfetta is grateful that *he* has forgiven *Lilia* (*A,* p. 65). Gino and his friend feel that they are gallant to waste so much time over women; and Forster, with impressive irony, causes the friend to sigh "dolefully, as if he found the nobility of his sex a burden" (*A,* p. 52).

Gino bemoans the difficulty of finding a *simpatica* woman (*A,* p. 51), and we must infer that life in Italy is hardly such as to give any woman the chance to become what he considers *simpatica.* It also gives him little opportunity to meet her if she does exist. He thinks that Caroline may be *simpatica,* and his attitude toward her compares interestingly with his attitude toward Lilia. At first he views Lilia as a superior being, but soon he sees her as sexual woman and therefore

inferior. He also views Caroline as superior, but since she
never reveals her sexuality to him, she is able to remain a
goddess. Caroline is in many ways a deeper and more sensitive person than Lilia, but we feel—and she knows—that if
she were to put herself into the role of wife in Italy, she
would be treated exactly as Lilia was. This puts Caroline
into a difficult position. She is attracted to Gino sexually,
but she knows that if he were aware of her feelings, he
would treat her miserably; the system in Italy assures this.
Therefore, although Caroline matures and is in some sense
saved by her recognition of sexual love, in the end she is
resigned to a sterile loneliness. Her only escape would be
Philip, but the system in England, with its strong, manipulative mothers, makes it impossible for *him,* a puppet, to respond sexually to her, to *live.* He in turn is saved by his discovery of brotherhood, but in this novel brotherhood and
sexuality cannot unite. Caroline can accept sexuality in Italy
and Philip can accept brotherhood there; but in Italy
brotherhood cannot exist for women and in England sexuality cannot exist for men. At the end of the book, Gino
becomes the love object for both Caroline and Philip, sexual
for one and companionate for the other. But the heterosexual love cannot be expressed or fulfilled, and the homosexual love is not perceived as physical.

Caroline's attraction to Gino is not unlikely. He is a contradictory character. On the one hand, he exhibits all that is
most wrong with Italian society in his attitude toward
women; but on the other hand, he exhibits all that is best in
the brotherhood that Philip discovers and the sexuality that
awakens Caroline. Our first piece of knowledge about him
defines him as "Italian nobility" (*A,* p. 19), and although this
claim is merely a snobbish attempt to get Sawston's approval
for Lilia's marriage, we later realize it has some truth in it.
Mrs. Herriton perceives the claim's implication that Gino
isn't noble, but we later discover that he possesses a natural
nobility unknown to her. Although he is both brutal and

mercenary toward Lilia, he is noble toward his son, "the first great passion of his life. Falling in love was a mere physical triviality" (*A*, p. 67); to him, a woman is merely a necessity for producing male children. He achieves greatness in the scene with the baby: "The man was majestic; he was a part of nature; in no ordinary love scene could he ever be so great" (*A*, p. 139).

Gino's attitude toward the physical care of the child places him squarely in the ranks of *machismo:* he likes to do things to take care of the baby, but those things "take up a good deal of time, and are not all suitable for a young man" (*A*, p. 136); so after Lilia's death, he decides to remarry to provide a mother for his son. We apparently cannot be told often enough that woman's most important role is that of mother, and Gino infuriates Caroline by asserting that his new wife "will do her duty well" (*A*, p. 135); of course, he never thinks of any duties of his own. He lists the qualifications of his new wife, and it sounds as if he were hiring a maid and a nurse rather than marrying a woman:

This woman will do exactly what I tell her. She is fond of children. She is clean; she has a pleasant voice. She is not beautiful; I cannot pretend that to you for a moment. But she is what I require.

[*A*, pp. 137–38]

After this catalogue, the baby gives a "piercing yell" (*A*, p. 138), and although his cry can be explained naturalistically by the fact that Gino is about to wash him, it functions symbolically as negative commentary on Gino's conception of what is necessary in a marriage.

It is irrational for Gino to be a sexual snob, to look down on women, for he is the victim of all the social snobbery in the book. One expects him to have some insight into the position of the underdog, but, like Aziz in *A Passage to India,* he doesn't make the connection. All the characters except Caroline look down on him. Lilia first presents herself as a

broad-minded democrat, but we soon realize that she is
both a social and a national snob: she condescends to Gino
personally (*A*, p. 43) and is horrified at the thought of an
"English child being educated at Monteriano" (*A*, p. 44).
Lilia is at the center of a neat symmetry: she patronizes and
condescends to Gino and all Italians just as Sawston and
Mrs. Herriton have patronized and condescended to her;
she is treated as a child by England and in turn treats Gino
as a boy. She never attempts to accept him as an equal; at
first she treats him as a pliable toy and then fears him as a
harsh master; she never sees him as just another person.
Their marriage is based on mutual snobbery, hers toward
the sons of Italian dentists and his toward women in general.

Philip is presented as a snob at first; worse yet, he is a
hypocritical snob who has seen and loved faces like Gino's
many times but who "did not want to see it opposite him at
dinner. It was not the face of a gentleman" (*A*, p. 31). He is
unable to accept the fact that Gino's father is a "dentist in
fairyland" (*A*, p. 26). However, Philip can ultimately overcome this and accept his brotherhood with Gino, thus tran-
scending class and defining himself as one of Forster's
"saved" characters.

Only Caroline is willing to overlook class difference from
the beginning, and this defines her as great, greater even
than Philip. Her belief that love can transcend social differences (*A*, p. 26) is noble, if inappropriate to Gino and
Lilia, who are hardly in love. Forster presents a similar attempt in *Howards End*, where Helen Schlegel tries to overcome social differences with sex; the result is not wholly
successful. Yet Forster clearly believes that these differences
can and must be overcome. Only in *Maurice* is class finally
transcended by combining sex and love.

Throughout *Where Angels Fear to Tread*, only two characters are consistently called by their last names. Philip, Gino,
Harriet, and Lilia are always called by first names only, but

Mrs. Herriton is always called Mrs. Herriton and Caroline is always Miss Abbott. These two women are the decision-makers, the most active characters, while the others for the most part are only acted upon. The use of Mrs. Herriton's last name has already been explored, but that of Miss Abbott's is more ambiguous. She is perhaps quintessential unmarried woman, as Mrs. Herriton is quintessential widow and mother; but this is unsatisfactory, for Harriet is also unmarried. The more likely explanation is that Forster wants us, the readers, to maintain a respectful distance from Miss Abbott, the hero and protagonist. We do not experience the same ironic intimacy with her that we have with Philip, Gino, Lilia, and Harriet.

In the first glimpse we have of Caroline, she is very much a part of Sawston society, surrounded by "numerous relatives" (*A*, p. 3); she is immediately contrasted with Lilia and emerges superior: "Miss Abbott, a tall, grave, rather nice-looking young lady . . . was conducting her adieus in a more decorous manner" (*A*, p. 4). After Caroline and Lilia leave for Italy, "poor Miss Abbott" becomes the topic of conversation at Mrs. Herriton's tea (*A*, p. 6); like "poor Isabella" in Jane Austen's *Emma,* this epithet reflects more on the narrowness of the judge than on the poverty of the judged. Caroline is to become much richer in knowledge by her companionship with Lilia and her trips to Italy. At this point, however, she still seems to fit in perfectly at Sawston; Mrs. Herriton approves of her (*A*, p. 11), and everyone is surprised that she wants to go to Italy (*A*, p. 22), that she wants to change. The "before" picture we get is of a woman young only chronologically, "good, quiet, dull, and amiable" (*A*, p. 21), who lives a life "devoted to dull acts of charity" (*A*, p. 83).

Caroline's first trip to Italy is traumatic and initiates her into adult responsibility. She blames herself for Lilia's marriage because she gives Lilia free choice, a freedom Lilia has never had in England; but Lilia's choice dooms her to vir-

tual slavery in Italy. Caroline is *not* truly responsible for
Lilia's plight, since she did not create the society and, indeed, had no idea that this is where the marriage would
lead. The situation is a failure for both women, since one
feels responsible when she is not, and the other, even when
presented with free choice, can choose only between being
oppressed indirectly or openly.

Caroline recognizes Lilia's oppression by the Herritons,
and when Philip implies that Lilia is incapable of choosing
her own happiness, Caroline challenges him: "Had you ever
let her choose?" (*A*, p. 75). Philip treats Lilia as a child, and
only Caroline recognizes her adulthood. She encourages
Lilia's marriage because she hates "the idleness, the stupid-
ity, the respectability, the petty unselfishness" (*A*, p. 76) of
Sawston.[7] Caroline admires Lilia for her vitality, the "power
of enjoying herself with sincerity" (*A*, p. 76) which she retains despite Sawston, and she hopes that Lilia will escape
Sawston's apathy. She soon realizes, however, that Lilia
"only changed one groove for another—a worse groove" (*A*,
p. 77).

Caroline originally intends to stay in Italy to supervise the
marriage and to carry with her Sawston's idea of the family,
for she wants to "influence" Gino (*A*, p. 75). Fortunately for
her future development, this does not work out, for Caroline is so distraught by the lie about Gino's "nobility" that
she loses her nerve and leaves with Philip. The lie which
becomes true, the claim of a nobility for Gino which he does
ultimately possess, keeps Caroline from falling into Sawston's traps even in Italy.

When she returns to "save" the baby, Caroline's approach
to life is still simplistic: "To her imagination Monteriano
had become a magic city of vice" (*A*, pp. 87–88); "She prepared to do battle with the powers of evil" (*A*, p. 127). Yet

7. Trilling, *Forster*, p. 67, points to this statement as a turning point: " 'Petty
unselfishness,' she insists and immediately becomes the heroine of the novel." I
would make one modification only: she becomes the hero.

she is much more complex than Lilia or Harriet, and in fact is so distressed at her realization that the situation will not fit her simple preconceptions that she wishes she were Harriet, a wish Philip interprets as "homage to the complexity of life" (*A,* p. 112). She has two distinct aspects, "the Miss Abbott who could travel alone to Monteriano, and the Miss Abbott who could not enter Gino's house when she got there" (*A,* p. 109)—Caroline the adventuresome person and Caroline the timid woman.

She feels responsible for the baby as soon as she hears of its existence, although Sawston thinks her mad for her interest (*A,* p. 85). She blames herself for Lilia's marriage and therefore for the birth of the child, but at first her concern is only for the *welfare* of the baby, which she sees as a "sacred duty" (*A,* p. 87), not for the baby himself. Disconcerted by the reality of the child, who is flesh and blood and not merely a principle (*A,* p. 130), she is even more disconcerted by the reality of Gino's love for his son: "The horrible truth, that wicked people are capable of love, stood naked before her, and her moral being was abashed" (*A,* p. 136). Again she wishes she were less complex, less sensitive to reality, and more rigid: "She longed for Harriet's burly obtuseness or for the soulless diplomacy of Mrs. Herriton" (*A,* p. 136); it is not easy to be a hero. She loses her "comfortable sense of virtue" and admits that she is "in the presence of something greater than right or wrong" (*A,* p. 137). Caroline takes the baby on her lap, and when Philip enters the room he sees, "to all intents and purposes, the Virgin and Child, with Donor" (*A,* p. 141). Unfortunately, Caroline's sensitivity is not enough to overcome society's constricted options for women, and fulfillment is denied her.[8]

Although she never achieves sexual fulfillment, Caroline does achieve sexual awareness. She likes Gino immediately

8. Trilling, ibid., p. 71, points out that "Gino is to be the Donor in more senses than one, but Miss Abbott is to remain a virgin."

(*A,* p. 25), before his marriage to Lilia, but by her second trip to Italy she has learned a lot from Lilia's experience and, taking up the cause of all women, forbids him to remarry: "You have ruined one woman; I forbid you to ruin another" (*A,* p. 133). She knows that he is only marrying to gain the services of a "housekeeper" and a "slave" (*A,* p. 135), and she is furious at him. However, when she is converted to the belief that he really loves the baby, she does pray to Santa Deodata, thus accepting woman's traditional passive role, although at this stage she does not necessarily love Gino. Bathing the baby, exhibiting "a woman's pleasure in cleaning" (*A,* p. 140), she seems to be following Lilia's path; she is saved only by her knowledge of what happens to Lilia and by the fact that Gino thinks of her as a goddess. After the baby's death, Philip too thinks of Caroline as a goddess, and she plays the role of mother to both men. Gino, in his sorrow, goes to Caroline like a child (*A,* p. 172), and both Gino and Philip obey her when she tells them to drink the child's milk, thus becoming united as brothers (*A,* p. 173). Because of her, they achieve communion, but her relationship with Gino does not continue beyond this; for this reason any hope for *her* future lies with Philip.

Caroline's education, which "inclined her to reverence the male" (*A,* p. 127), forces her to react to Philip first as a man and only then as a person, which inhibits the development of a mature, connected relationship between them. Still, to Philip alone Caroline confides at the end that she loves Gino sexually: "I'm in love with Gino . . . I mean it crudely—you know what I mean" (*A,* p. 181). Philip at first cannot conceive of Caroline's love for Gino as sexual and equates it with his own love for Gino. In the light of *Maurice,* this may be more accurate than he knows. Caroline, at any rate, does perceive the nature of her own love for Gino and insists that she is not ashamed of it, although if this were really true she would not equate sexuality with crudity. She fears and represses her sexual nature throughout the early part of the book; when she sees Gino alone, before she first sees the baby, she is terrified and screams (*A,* p. 129). Only at the end of the novel do we realize, when she does, that her scream was one of terror at her own sexuality, a sexuality expressed in the recurring image of a smoke ring that envelopes her (*A,* pp. 129; 183). She insists to Philip that she is not refined, and she is right. She is not a lady; she is a woman, willing to acknowledge her own sexuality: "He's not a gentleman, nor a Christian, nor good in any way. He's never flattered me nor honoured me. But because he's handsome, that's been enough" (*A,* p. 181). That she confides to a *man,* "who might understand and not be disgusted," what she could not bear to tell a *woman* (*A,* p. 180), implies that men are more tolerant of sexuality than women, a point reiterated in *A Room with a View.* In *Where Angels Fear to Tread,* ironically and rather sadly, Philip the man is not disgusted by the sexuality of others, but Philip the product of a manipulative mother is incapable of any sexuality of his own.

Whether Caroline's salvation is worth the price is questionable: Gino's worship of her may have doomed her to a life of sterility and loneliness. Her role as traditional, passive woman keeps *her* from declaring her love to him, thus unfortunately preventing her from experiencing sex but also keeping her from the degrading role of an Italian wife. Philip provides no real alternative, since he also worships Caroline. Incapable of sexuality, he cannot make her life transcendent, merely "endurable" (*A,* p. 184); and she asserts correctly that "All the wonderful things are over" (*A,* p. 179). The book ends with Caroline's separation from Gino: although the sexuality of Italy is attractive, marriage in Italy is so oppressive as to be impossible. There is no physical separation from Philip, but there is certainly no union either; although marriage to an Englishman is a possibility, a sexual relationship with this Englishman is not,

and therefore Caroline is left with no chance for fulfillment—a very modern ending for a very modern book. As
Forster states in his 1907 essay, "Pessimism in Literature,"
marriage is no longer an end for women, nor for their husbands; so it is no longer possible to end a modern book with
a marriage.[9] Yet Forster does not always abide by his own
rules: only two of his six novels end with separations (*Where
Angels Fear to Tread* and *A Passage to India*),[10] while three
end with marriage or the equivalent (*A Room with a View,
Howards End,* and *Maurice*), and one ends with the death of
the protagonist, the most final of separations, while his
brother goes on to marriage and a child (*The Longest Journey*).

Philip's relations with women throughout the book are affected by the fact that he is totally dominated by his mother.
He is a puppet who can criticize but not rebel (*A,* p. 87), and
he even enjoys his mother's "diplomacy," with the result
that he does "not think of his own morals and behaviour
any more" (*A,* p. 82). He reflects his mother's conde-
scending attitude toward Lilia; when he goes to Italy to try
to prevent her marriage, he says to her, "I know everything" (*A,* p. 33), a statement that assures us he knows very
little. We are given no physical description of Philip until
rather late in the book, after Lilia's death (*A,* p. 68). The
news of her death reaches Sawston on Philip's twenty-
fourth birthday, implying that Philip can only be reborn at
Lilia's expense. His eventual "salvation," such as it is, comes
about through his recognition of brotherhood, but it is the
brotherhood of *men,* Italian style, achieved only at the expense of women; it is for this reason that his birthday is
Lilia's death day.

Philip is romantic, in a pejorative sense (*A,* p. 26), toward

9. E. M. Forster, "Pessimism in Literature," in *Albergo Empedocle and other writings,*
ed. George H. Thomson (New York, Liveright, 1971), p. 135.
10. There is a marriage at the end of *A Passage to India,* but it is secondary to the
separation of the principals; Stella suddenly appears at the end of the novel and is
rather peripheral.

both places and people, and his attitude toward women is patronizing and protective, the negative side of chivalry. It does not change greatly throughout the novel, although he does develop in other ways and outgrows his early national and class snobbery. Perhaps because of his mother's influence, or perhaps because of his romantic chivalry, he seems unable to express any hostility or resentment directly *to* women, but only impersonally *at* women: " 'Tear each other's eyes out!' he cried, gesticulating at the façade of the hotel. 'Give it to her, Harriet! . . . Give it to her, Caroline! . . . Go it, ladies; go it!' " (*A*, p. 103). His early relationship with Caroline reflects his general attitude toward women; he imputes to her an inferior intelligence, "the usual feminine incapacity for grasping philosophy" (*A*, p. 78). Even when he falls in love with her, it is for the wrong reason: "The gush of sentimentalism . . . made her more alluring" (*A*, p. 148). What Philip sees as mere feminine emotionalism is rather sensitivity and acute perceptiveness, for Caroline is the only character who is able to realize, accurately, that Gino does love his child.

Caroline's insight includes Philip in its scope as well as Gino. She shows herself to be more alive and more beautiful than he is when she rejects as blasphemous his sterile detachment (*A*, p. 153), for she "really cared about life, and tried to live it properly" (*A*, p. 112). She sadly recognizes Philip's deadness, attributing it to his mother's influence:

You appreciate us all—see good in all of us. And all the time you are dead-dead-dead. . . . You are so splendid . . . that I can't bear to see you wasted. I can't bear—she has not been good to you—your mother.

[*A*, pp. 150–51]

Philip's unlived life is Jamesian in its thoroughness.[11] His self-awareness is nil when, at the precise moment that he

11. Trilling, *Forster*, p. 73, points out that Philip reminds us of the hero of "The Beast in the Jungle."

falls in love with Caroline, he asserts that he is not falling in love (*A*, p. 151) and thus kills any chance for the love to be reciprocated.

After Philip rejects this symbolic moment and denies his love for Caroline, his life becomes "unreal" (*A*, p. 159), just as in *The Longest Journey* Rickie's life becomes unreal when he misses a similar symbolic moment and rejects brotherhood for the sake of an unworthy woman. Philip, however, does finally regain reality if not the (worthy) woman when he accepts the responsibilities as well as the pleasures of brotherhood, blames himself for the baby's death, and takes the news to Gino (*A*, p. 166). He now thinks that he is very much in love with Caroline, although his love is minimally physical, and even that much only because Gino reminds him that the physical exists (*A*, p. 176). We cannot help feeling that if Philip were able to love Caroline sexually as well as spiritually and worshipfully, the novel would end differently. The essentially non-physical mother-worship that Philip calls love is apparently all he is capable of, and we must agree with Caroline that his mother has not been good to him. His worship of Caroline as a goddess who "stood outside all degradation" (*A*, p. 184) anticipates Clive's relationship with Anne in *Maurice* and is just as chilling. Philip does not tell Caroline that he loves her; he is passive, like Santa Deodata and like Caroline with Gino. But they are women and have been taught to be passive; no such societal explanation exists for Philip: this is clearly the final, dreadful outcome of his mother's manipulation. Forster's later books attribute male passivity to "undeveloped hearts" [12] produced by the British public school system.

There still remains one important character, another character whom Mrs. Herriton manipulates and whom Philip patronizes: Harriet. Because the novel ends with

---

12. E. M. Forster, "Notes on the English Character," in *Abinger Harvest* (New York, Harcourt, Brace, 1936), p. 5.

Harriet's vision, an analysis of Harriet will appropriately end this study of the novel. In her role as the representative of the English suburban system, she is unaffected by either Italian sexuality or Italian brotherhood; "always unfortunate" (*A*, p. 121), she is repelled by Italy in a series of symbolic insults: her sketch book is stolen; ammonia is spilled on her prayer book; she loses her crochet in Florence; she is hit on the chest by a bouquet at the opera; and, as the novel closes, Philip and Caroline "hurried back to the carriage to close the windows lest the smuts should get in Harriet's eyes" (*A*, p. 184).

A simple and generally unsympathetic character, Harriet does contribute one major insight after Lilia's death: "The whole thing is like one of those horrible modern plays where no one is in the right" (*A*, p. 70). This comment relates to the title of the novel, *Where Angels Fear to Tread,* and we must ask if Harriet is correct, if *no one* is in the right, and all the characters are indeed fools rushing in. This does seem to be the case; they all do seem foolish, in different ways, and their attempts to deal with things beyond their comprehension lead only to a great deal of harm and to two incomplete salvations. Harriet herself, despite this insight, achieves no salvation at all and does only harm.

It is almost too easy to describe Harriet; she is inflexible, virtuous, fanatically and narrowly religious, materialistic, boring, simplistic, and wholly impervious to her surroundings: "acrid, indissoluble, large; the same in Italy as in England—changing her disposition never, and her atmosphere under protest" (*A*, p. 114). Harriet is unwilling to be swayed from her preconceived ideas by reality and finds it "Disgusting!" (*A*, p. 145) that Caroline washes the baby; Caroline is infinitely the more sympathetic character, if only because she is more open to experience and therefore more alive. Harriet considers Caroline a "turnncoat" and a "coward" for allowing herself to develop and change (*A*, p. 151); and she levels against her that worst of all possible charges, that she is not a lady (*A*, p. 143). According to Harriet, Caroline as a "lady" must be severely circumscribed in her actions, and in this Harriet speaks for both British and Italian society. The demand that women be ladies is discussed in most of Forster's books, and especially in *A Room with a View*.

Harriet is not completely to be despised, however; she *is* "a straight, brave woman" (*A*, p. 99), and she does allow herself to be moved by one external force: Lilia's diary. She breaks out of her role as representative of Sawston society in only this one instance, and significantly this instance involves the plight of all women. Harriet is kept awake nights by the thought of Lilia's suffering and allows herself to react as a woman, to sympathize and identify with another woman's fate (*A*, p. 70). However, her interpretation of Lilia's situation differs markedly from ours, for to Harriet Gino's primary sin is his infidelity, which defines him as a "man who is unchivalrous to a woman" (*A*, p. 98) and therefore totally evil. This evaluation, like her demand that women be "ladies," places her clearly back on the side of conventional society, whereas Forster implies that it is not lack of chivalry but rather lack of consideration for another *person's* feelings which is the ultimate evil.

Harriet represents the antilife sterility of English society in her lack of affinity for Gino and Lilia's child; it is ultimately *her* action that leads to his death. She steals and drops the baby and, at the moment of catastrophe, bursts out laughing (*A*, pp. 163–64); Sawston triumphs, but in an ambiguous way. We never know the details of Harriet's "crime" nor her exact motivation (*A*, p. 165); all we know for certain is that Harriet and her mother never realize the transcendence of what happens (*A*, pp. 177–78) and therefore do not attain even the limited salvation offered to Philip and Caroline. Feminine, philistine England cannot tolerate masculinity, and must destroy the son produced by masculine, philistine Italy. The daughter produced earlier by feminine England, the child Irma, survives but is doomed at the end of the novel to repeat the cycle, to grow up ignorant and thus become a philistine herself, a Mrs. Herriton, a Harriet, or a Lilia, whose warning she is not allowed to hear.

Two
The Longest Journey

If marriage is a prison for women in *Where Angels Fear to Tread,* it is a prison for both sexes in *The Longest Journey,* but especially for men. It cuts them off from brotherhood and friendship, particularly the friendship with homosexual overtones we have seen between Philip and Gino in *Where Angels Fear to Tread,* which is the norm in Italian *caffè* life. *The Longest Journey* contrasts friendship with marriage; Rickie's relationship with Ansell, his friend from Cambridge, is stronger and obviously deeper than his relationship with his wife, Agnes. A writer, Rickie avers that "in literature we needn't intrude our own limitations," [1] in reference to a story he has written about a happy marriage. If *The Longest Journey* is indeed autobiographical, as many critics have suggested, we may understand this to be the early statement of a homosexual author who chooses to write about marriage, both happy and unhappy, in most of his books. Although it was Forster's favorite,[2] it is one of his least successful novels; the lack of control, detachment, and irony that we find in it and in *Maurice,* also an autobiographical novel, relates to the fact that in these two works males are the protagonists and women play a relatively unimportant role.

1. E. M. Forster, *The Longest Journey* (New York, Vintage paperback, n.d.), p. 296. All future references to this work will follow the pagination of this readily available edition and will appear in the text in the abbreviated form *LJ*.
2. E. M. Forster, "A View Without a Room: Old Friends Fifty Years Later," *New York Times Book Review,* July 27, 1958, p. 4.

Brotherhood in *The Longest Journey* first emerges at Cambridge; Agnes learns early in the novel that Rickie's friends are like brothers to him, but she replies, "He has no real brothers" (*LJ*, p. 9). "Fratribus," the dedication and perhaps also an epigraph to the novel, is precisely what Rickie must discover. Although Stephen, his illegitimate half brother, knows fraternity intuitively (*LJ*, p. 262), Rickie is unable to accept him or his knowledge of true brotherhood, for Rickie insists on idealizing and labeling people rather than seeing them as individuals—his one great fault, which finally destroys him. Rickie is lame, and his deformity is the inability to walk with his brother. As a child he reminds us of the young Maurice, lonely and different: "Shall I ever have a friend? . . . I don't see how. They walk too fast. And a brother I shall never have" (*LJ*, p. 26). Rickie ultimately has Ansell as a friend and Stephen as a brother, yet his deformity keeps him from really connecting with them; he chooses instead the unreality of marriage to Agnes.

Rickie is aware of the "irony of friendship":

so strong it is, and so fragile. We fly together, like straws in an eddy, to part in the open stream. Nature has no use for us: she has cut her stuff differently. Dutiful sons, loving husbands, responsible fathers—these are what she wants, and if we are friends it must be in our spare time.

[*LJ*, p. 69]

Ansell's reaction to this and similar beliefs states Forster's great theme, the acceptance of individual differentness: "The point is, not what's ordained by nature or any other fool, but what's right" (*LJ*, p. 87). Ansell tells Rickie to react to people spontaneously, as individuals, rather than as images (*LJ*, p. 21), but Rickie does not take his advice: "he wished there was a society, a kind of friendship office, where the marriage of true minds could be registered" (*LJ*, p. 69). He wants to label his relationship with Ansell, but labeling has only negative results. While the novel stresses again and again the dangers of labeled marriage, it also touches briefly on the perils of a labeled friendship when Ansell and Rickie are cavorting in a meadow, almost as lovers: Ansell jealously "held him prisoner" (*LJ*, p. 70) to stop him from going to see Agnes.

The title of *The Longest Journey* comes from Shelley's *Epipsychidion*,[3] a poem with the theme that marriage drastically limits one's horizons:

> "*I never was attached to that great sect*
> *Whose doctrine is that each one should select*
> *Out of the world a mistress or a friend,*
> *And all the rest, though fair and wise, commend*
> *To cold oblivion,—though it is the code*
> *Of modern morals, and the beaten road*
> *Which those poor slaves with weary footsteps tread*
> *Who travel to their home among the dead*
> *By the broad highway of the world,—and so*
> *With one sad friend, perhaps a jealous foe,*
> *The dreariest and the longest journey go.*"
>
> [*LJ*, p. 138]

In *The Longest Journey*, marriage is totally destructive not only of fraternity but also of one's ability to accept the significance of symbolic moments, a rejection which inevitably leads to a loss of reality. Marriage, unlike friendship, is an attempt to locate one's reality in someone else,[4] a futile and destructive ambition. Although Rickie is the protagonist, he is not a hero. His situation is that of many modern men and women: out of touch with reality and overwhelmed by forces he does not understand. Only an occasional hero like Ansell or a born countryman like Stephen manages to escape.[5]

Fraternity is first extended beyond Cambridge to the lower class, through a few comic but important comments

3. Trilling, *Forster*, p. 81.
4. Herbert Howarth, lecture, University of Pennsylvania, Nov. 1, 1967.
5. Ibid.

about bedmakers. Later Stephen, Rickie's real, blood
brother, extends it even further, for he is the product of a
mixed-class union and is of no class himself. Forster's
greater stress on the general brotherhood of men and not
on the blood relationship of Rickie and Stephen reempha-
sizes his belief that arbitrary class distinctions must be overcome. Rickie, truly egalitarian toward the bedders at Cambridge, blames them as much as gentlefolk "for the present
lamentable state of things" (*LJ*, p.60); and Stephen, truly
democratic, treats shepherds as equals and demands full
repayment of debts from them. He refuses to patronize
lower-class characters, as Agnes and Mrs. Failing do.

Our judgment of the Pembrokes is influenced by their
treatment of the lower classes. When we first meet Herbert,
he is rude to Mrs. Aberdeen, the bedmaker (*LJ*, p. 11);
Agnes, who is still likable, reprimands him. Later, however,
Agnes shows herself to be a snob and insults Ansell's sister
for the heinous crime of being the daughter of a draper
(*LJ*, p. 214). Agnes's snobbery is integrally related to her
rejection of Stephen and brotherhood.

The Longest Journey concerns itself with the social situation
in much the same way as *Man and Superman,* which was written four years earlier. John Tanner sums up his philosophy
neatly in *The Revolutionist's Handbook,* a remarkable docu-
ment: "Do not waste your time on Social Questions. What is
the matter with the poor is Poverty; what is the matter with
the rich is Uselessness." [6] This is a nice comment on the
relationship of socialism to the philosophical question of the
reality of the real world. Indeed, only the rich can worry
about reality; the poor are only too aware that it exists.[7]
Like Shaw, Forster disapproves of the class system, and
especially of the existence of parasitic "gentlemen": Ansell's
money is "alive" as compared to Rickie's, which is "dead"
(*LJ*, p. 33). Rickie wishes that he were not "a cumbersome
gentleman" (*LJ*, p. 139), and he respects the lower-class

6. Shaw, *Man and Superman,* p. 270.   7. Howarth, Nov. 1, 1967.

lovers who are able to marry on much less money than he has, while he must wait.

The lower-class characters in both works are impressive; the pride and detachment of the chauffeur and the bedder are beautifully drawn. Forster asserts that

Bedmakers have to be comic and dishonest. It is expected of them. In a picture of university life it is their only function. So when we meet one who has the face of a lady, and feelings of which a lady might be proud, we pass her by.

[*LJ*,p. 10]

Forster tells us to react to lower-class women as if they were ladies, but unlike the books with female protagonists, *The Longest Journey* does not take this idea one step further. It does not tell us to react to both women and ladies, regardless of class, as if they were people.

Women are integrally involved in the tension between reality and unreality at the heart of *The Longest Journey*. In the undergraduate discussions at Cambridge in this novel, a cow epitomizes reality, and we must infer that Forster uses a cow because a cow is female.[8] Ironically, she is alive, unlike Rickie's mother and daughter; she is in touch with nature, unlike Mrs. Failing; and she is "real," unlike Agnes. Of course she is also subhuman, but that does not seem to mitigate against her at all.

Ansell insists that Agnes is not real, that she does not exist (*LJ*, p. 18), but to Rickie "She had more reality than any other woman in the world" (*LJ*, p. 51). She does not have more reality than any other "person" in the world, however, and we are forced to question the reality of all women. Agnes's inability to acknowledge the dead, "whose images alone have immortality" (*LJ*, p. 182) to Rickie, contributes to her unreality. Rickie unfortunately does not realize that his idealization of the dead makes him unable to consider Ste-

8. Trilling, *Forster*, p. 77, finds this an unusual image: "they have chosen a cow as example, rather than the table consecrated to such discussions."

phen, a living human being, as real (*LJ*, p. 191). He explains his feeling of unreality at Sawston as "nothing more than a feeling that the cow was not really there. [Agnes] laughed, and 'How is the cow today?' soon passed into a domestic joke" (*LJ*, p. 191).

Man and Superman is again relevant, for its insert, "Don Juan in Hell," comments directly on the problem of reality and unreality, heaven and hell; in Shaw's hell, the "horror of damnation" is that "Nothing is real," [9] while "heaven is the home of the masters of reality." [10] Don Juan reminds us of the way Ansell perceives Rickie's life with Agnes when he describes the Shavian hell:

Here you call your appearance beauty, your emotions love, your sentiments heroism, your aspirations virtue, just as you did on earth; but here there are no hard facts to contradict you, no ironic contrast of your needs with your pretensions, no human comedy, nothing but a perpetual romance, a universal melodrama.[11]

The pathos of Rickie's life proves Juan's point that earth is "the home of the slaves of reality." [12] Forster's conception of heaven is Shavian in nature, although to him reality is more closely bound up with the natural world: "If the dell was to bear any inscription, he would have liked it to be 'this way to Heaven,' . . . and he did not realize till later years that the number of visitors would not thereby have sensibly increased" (*LJ*, p. 20). Rickie's deterioration results from the fact that "he was frightened at reality; he was frightened at the splendours and horrors of the world" (*LJ*, p. 64). Rickie at Sawston is in a Shavian hell, and he "prayed to be delivered from the shadow of unreality that had begun to darken the world" (*LJ*, p. 165). Forster's hell, like Shaw's, is connected with women: Agnes, "like the world she created for [Rickie], was unreal" (*LJ*, p. 203); after he leaves her, he

9. Shaw, *Man and Superman*, p. 130.   10. Ibid., p. 142.
11. Ibid.   12. Ibid.

is able to assert triumphantly that "the cow is there. The world is real again" (*LJ*, p. 297).

Stewart Ansell, a figure of enlightenment, speaks the first words in the novel when he says, "The cow is there" (*LJ*, p. 1), and he lights a match as he speaks.[13] The match becomes a pervasive image for him, and the word "match" can be defined as "union," a concept about which Ansell has many theories. Clearly, Ansell rather than Agnes is Rickie's proper match; but on a realistic level, the match goes out. Its light is temporary, implying that no one is anyone's permanent match, that marriage is not a viable institution. When Rickie announces his engagement to Agnes, the atmosphere is unreal and Ansell is silent: "He was no match for these two quite clever women" (*LJ*, p. 84). This sentence works three ways: (1) his influence over Rickie does not equal theirs, the most obvious reading; (2) he is not a source of enlightenment for *them;* and (3) he is not heterosexual and therefore not susceptible to an engagement himself.[14]

Forster's sympathies always lie with the underdog and the outsider—one reason his women are so impressive—and Ansell, as a Jew with a homosexual temperament, surely qualifies. Yet Ansell, whom we would expect to identify with women, is a misogynist. We must reject his misogyny at the same time that we accept his reasons for it. He is correct in his estimation of Agnes as personally neither serious nor truthful (*LJ*, p. 89), and his definition of a "lady" as essentially manipulative (*LJ*, p. 86) is accurate in Forster's world; but he is not enlightened enough to see that women are as trapped and destroyed by being ladylike as are the men they manipulate. Yet Ansell declares war on women (*LJ*, p. 87), and we may attribute this partly to a possible homosexual jealousy.

13. Howarth, Nov. 1, 1967.
14. Frederick Crews, *E. M. Forster: The Perils of Humanism* (Princeton, Princeton University Press, 1962), p. 56, implies the last reading when he attributes Ansell's misgivings about marriage to "a basically homosexual temperament."

Ansell's argument against Rickie's marriage has two aspects, the personal and the general. The first convinces; the second does not. Ansell is sure that the couple's happiness will not last, and he predicts that Agnes will eventually long for "a jollier husband" (*LJ,* p. 87). But he does not blame her for this, thus underscoring *Rickie's* uniqueness: Agnes is simply mismatched. During Rickie's engagement, Ansell writes him a telling letter:

You are not a person who ought to marry at all. You are unfitted in body. . . . You are also unfitted in soul: you want and you need to like many people, and a man of that sort ought not to marry.

[*LJ,* p. 88]

Ansell's personal objection, that Rickie is unfit in body, refers not only to his lameness, but to his latent homosexuality as well.[15]

Ansell's general objection, that Rickie is unfit in soul to marry, is extended to imply that no one should marry, and he quotes Shelley to Rickie: " 'You never were attached to that great sect' who can like one person only, and if you try to enter it you will find destruction" (*LJ,* p. 88). The end of Ansell's letter asserts his belief that Rickie is "extraordinarily civilized" (*LJ,* p. 88), a phrase equated in this novel with liking not only one person, not with being homosexual, as we might infer. We see in *Maurice* that Maurice wants *a* friend, not many friends; he is devoted first to Clive, then

15. Crews, *Perils of Humanism,* p. 57, supports this interpretation when he states that Rickie "is not, strictly speaking, a homosexual, but his physical handicap and his effeminacy are such that the more genuine strains of homosexuality in Ansell strike a responsive chord in him." Wilfred Stone, *The Cave and the Mountain: A Study of E. M. Forster* (Stanford, Stanford University Press, 1966), p. 193, acutely analyzes Rickie's sexual dilemma: "This latent homosexuality is one of the realities of his nature. He must either courageously face this knowledge and its consequences or else try to force his life into an alien, conventional mold. . . . Either way, he faces a test—the one of his courage to defy convention, the other of his courage to endure it." Rickie makes the second choice; in *Maurice,* Maurice makes the first.

to Alec, one at a time. Ansell's use of Shelley's word "sect" implies a religious view of sexuality that anticipates Clive's religious Hellenism.

Ansell's general objections to marriage sound strongly Shavian: his letter states that "Man wants to love mankind; woman wants to love one man. When she has him her work is over. She is the emissary of Nature, and Nature's bidding has been fulfilled" (*LJ*, p. 88).[16] Agnes is indeed a derivative of Ann, and Shaw himself asserts that "every woman is not Ann, but Ann is Everywoman."[17] John Tanner recognizes Ann's power, and might well be speaking for Rickie when he cries, "we're beaten—smashed—nonentitized";[18] Tanner's perception is close to Ansell's when he warns Tavy about "the devilish side of a woman's fascination: she makes you will your own destruction"[19] and he seems to be thinking of Shelley's poem when he asks, "do they allow us any purpose [or] freedom of our own? Will they lend us to one another? Can the strongest man escape from them when once he is appropriated?"[20] He sees men as victims of female manipulation and accuses Ann of "that damnable woman's trick of heaping obligations on a man, of placing yourself so entirely and helplessly at his mercy that at last he dare not take a step without running to you for leave."[21] Ansell, speaking of Agnes, might be speaking of Ann when he says, "She is happy because she has conquered" (*LJ*, p. 87).

At Sawston Rickie loses his independence as inevitably as Tanner is about to at the end of the play, but Rickie is not being used by the Life Force, as Tanner is. In fact, we rec-

---

16. K. W. Gransden, *E. M. Forster* (Edinburgh and London, Oliver and Boyd, 1962), p. 39, sees marriage in *The Longest Journey* as "a conventional weapon of the Shavian life-force," and Ansell's letter arouses Wilfred Stone's suspicion, *Cave and the Mountain*, p. 199, "that he has recently been reading *Man and Superman*." Stone, ibid., p. 410*n*35, goes further to state that "Agnes Pembroke is the same blind carrier of the Life Force as Ann Whitefield."
17. Shaw, *Man and Superman*, p. xxix.   18. Ibid., p. 60.
19. Ibid., p. 61.   20. Ibid., p. 62.   21. Ibid., pp. 76–77.

ognize Rickie's genius most clearly when he tells Agnes to mind Gerald's death, when he realizes that her Life Force has been destroyed. Rickie himself has no physical contact with the Life Force, and his baby dies:

Henceforward he deteriorates. . . . He has lost the work that he loved, his friends, and his child. He remained conscientious and decent, but the spiritual part of him proceeded towards ruin.

[*LJ*, pp. 209–10]

Rickie should not have married, according to Shaw's theory; for his deformity, in the sense that he is a gentleman, places him against the evolution of a Superman, and the fact that he is an artist irrevocably alienates him from productive marriage. Shaw seems to be speaking of both Rickie and Ansell when he states that "Whether the artist becomes poet or philosopher . . . his sexual doctrine is nothing but a barren special pleading for pleasure, excitement, and knowledge when he is young, and for contemplative tranquillity when he is old and satiated"; [22] significantly, Ann's name for the character who wants to be an artist in *Man and Superman* is "*Ricky*-Ticky-Tavy."

Ansell accepts Shaw's theories too completely. He does not realize that both men and women are oppressed by arbitrary sex roles and conventions; he can sympathize only with men. When he calls woman "the emissary of Nature," he does not take into account his own great comment that what matters is not nature "but what's right." He assumes that men want civilization but women do not:

man does not care a damn for Nature—or at least only a very little damn. He cares for a hundred things besides, and the more civilized he is the more he will care for these hundred other things, and demand not only a wife and children, but also friends, and work, and spiritual freedom.

[*LJ*, p. 88]

22. Ibid., p. xxi.

By equating "civilized" with masculine and "natural" with feminine, Ansell arbitrarily cuts off half of woman's possibilities, a view which fortunately is transcended in *Howards End,* a novel with, significantly, a female protagonist. In *Howards End,* women too "demand not only a [husband] and children, but also friends, and work, and spiritual freedom." In *The Longest Journey,* Ansell sees woman as merely body, like that cow, and reproduction as woman's only role; in *Howards End* it is one of many roles. In *The Longest Journey* it is not essential for men to want to reproduce physically; in *Howards End* it is also nonessential for women. Helen chooses to do so; Margaret does not. Reproduction becomes a matter of choice, not of duty, and both sexes are thereby humanized.

Ansell's argument against Rickie's marrying could be made much more impressive and still remain within the philosophical framework of *Man and Superman* if he abandoned Shaw's arbitrary sex roles and addressed himself instead to Rickie as artist. In this area Agnes is most purely negative: "she had always mistrusted the little stories" (*LJ*, p. 165). Because of her, Rickie accepts a job he hates at a school he hates and never becomes a major creative force. Ansell's generalizations about women deceive him, for Rickie as artist is much more closely linked to nature than Agnes as woman: his stories all deal with Pan and Dryads and what he deprecatingly refers to as the "ridiculous idea of getting into touch with Nature" (*LJ*, p. 78). The one story whose plot we're told is almost a paradigm of what happens to Rickie and Agnes:

a stupid vulgar man is engaged to a lovely young lady. He wants her to live in the towns, but she only cares for woods. She shocks him this way and that, but gradually he tames her, and makes her almost as dull as he is. One day she has a last explosion . . . and flies out of the drawing-room window, shouting, 'Freedom and truth!'

[*LJ*, p. 77]

The sex roles in the novel itself are reversed: the woman entraps the man. Rickie does not make the connection and therefore does not escape, but Forster does connect and identifies Rickie with the woman protagonist. That Forster actually wrote the story described, "Other Kingdom," reinforces our belief that Forster as artist (and possibly Forster as homosexual) is able to identify with women, see their points of view, and thus present them sympathetically.

Ansell's view of marriage, while the most important one presented in *The Longest Journey*, is not the only one: Rickie and Agnes have their own attitudes, different both from Ansell's and from each other's. We discover Agnes's peculiar idea of marriage very early in the novel, long before we consider her a possible match for Rickie. The image of her earrings links marriage to ritual mutilation; they are "her only freak" (*LJ*, p. 7), something she has always wanted but does not get until Gerald proposes. Gerald, sharing her view of marriage, buys her the primitive "little gold knobs, copied, the jeweller told them, from something prehistoric" (*LJ*, p. 8); after she has her ears pierced, Gerald kisses "the spots of blood on her handkerchief" (*LJ*, p. 8). This ear-piercing ceremony, a sexual deflowering, is the closest Agnes and Gerald come to consummating their love, but it is more real than anything Agnes ever achieves with Rickie. Agnes feels that her earrings represent her uniqueness; she asserts that she is "not like other girls" (*LJ*, p. 8). When she marries Rickie, she gives up both her earrings and her uniqueness, for it and they are intimately tied up with Gerald; in this as in every other sense, the Agnes who marries Rickie is not the same woman he has idealized in her embrace with her proper match.

Rickie's early views on marriage, inspired by Cambridge and Ansell, are apparent in his reaction to Agnes's engagement to Gerald. He does not congratulate her, saying that he knows nothing about marriage (*LJ*, p. 13). Yet Rickie's attitude toward Agnes and Gerald's love affair becomes stronger than anything he ever feels for Agnes herself; he witnesses an embrace between them and through it experiences his first awareness of the power of sex. In effect, he falls in love with love, and he falls in love with them. His attempt to give them the money that would enable them to marry is angrily but correctly interpreted by Gerald to Agnes as evidence of Rickie's desire to marry both of them himself: "Marry us—he, you, and me" (*LJ*, p. 53). Rickie would have made a better mentor than husband, but that role is denied him.

Forster attributes to chance the fact that Rickie is overwhelmed, in a positive sense, by a heterosexual embrace: "It was the merest accident that Rickie had not been disgusted. But this he could not know" (*LJ*, p. 43). We know, however, and our knowledge colors our reaction to all that follows. Significantly, Rickie limps away from the love scene (*LJ*, p. 43); his deformity, not often stressed, takes on special importance after his vision of heterosexual physical love.

Rickie's understanding of his vision is not at all realistic. He sees Agnes and Gerald as transfigured, as "priest and high priestess" (*LJ*, p. 44) rather than real people, and this prepares us for Rickie's later inability to see Stephen as real. Rickie's main fault, idealizing people and imputing to them feelings and value they don't possess, is nowhere more destructive than here. It even affects his art, for in his stories he "deflected his enthusiasms" (*LJ*, p. 65) away from nature and toward heterosexual love. As Rickie at the end of the novel is to use his imagination to write about a happy marriage, so here he must use his imagination to write about heterosexual physical love, something else he has not experienced at first hand.

Rickie's deterioration is assured even earlier in the novel than his marriage to Agnes, for his very attraction to the brutal, negative aspects of both sexes [23] rather than to their

23. Lionel Trilling's brilliant insight into Rickie's attitude toward Agnes and Gerald, *Forster*, p. 89, is extremely helpful here: "Indeed, although the novelist

loving and positive sides is necessarily fatal. Ansell's alternative provides no real aid. He merely attributes all good to men and all bad to women, an equally simplistic and arbitrary solution. Rickie's problem is deeper than it seems: he is not simply a heterosexual man who marries the wrong woman for the wrong reasons, and he is not simply a homosexual man who destroys himself by attempting a heterosexual life. He is rather a sexually ambivalent man who commits himself totally to one (perhaps the wrong) sex, and a philosophically ambivalent man who commits himself totally to the wrong values.

Gerald is a sexual and a class snob; he cannot stand talking to servants, especially when the servant in question is a woman who is not pretty (*LJ*, pp. 41–42). Yet the particular ugly cook he abhors cries at the news of his death (*LJ*, p. 56), as do the other servants: "They had not liked Gerald, but he was a man, they were women, he had died" (*LJ*, pp. 56–57). The respect tendered the ruling sex and class by the "inferior" sex and class is not reciprocated. Gerald is brutal and considers brutality a mark of manliness; he thinks it "Woman's job" (*LJ*, p. 53) to pity the weak, to be humane. His sudden death in a football match is appropriate to his view of polarized sexuality, a "masculine" end for a "masculine" man. But as he dies he becomes human rather than "masculine"; he cries like a child, and we can sympathize

does not say so, we can almost imagine that Rickie was in love not so much with the girl herself as with her 'manly' and brutal lover, in love in the sense that he was identifying himself with the strong and dominant man by marrying [Agnes] . . . ; Agnes with her gay talk of horsewhipping, her pleasure at the idea of the weak boy in the hands of the strong boy, was Gerald's counterpart." James McConkey, *The Novels of E. M. Forster* (Ithaca, N. Y.: Cornell University Press, 1957), p. 37, also sees Agnes as another Gerald, "brutal and masculine," and, p. 34, compares Rickie's attraction to virility to Helen Schlegel's in *Howards End*. Patricia Edgerton's construct is even more useful, for in her excellent essay, "The Androgynous Mind: A Consideration of E. M. Forster and Virginia Woolf," (unpublished M.A. thesis, Columbia University, 1956, p. 50, she sees Agnes as the unpleasant side of the eternal feminine and Gerald as the unpleasant side of the eternal masculine, both without any inkling that masculine and feminine could possibly have anything in common. Significantly, Gerald and Agnes share this polarized view of sexuality with Stewart Ansell.

with him for the first and only time.[24] "I shan't do as a spirit," he sighs pathetically (*LJ*, p. 56), and he is correct: purely physical, Gerald cannot be a powerful enough spirit to keep Agnes from deteriorating or from using Rickie to take his place.

The marriage between Rickie and Agnes is a catastrophe. We see this early when Forster announces ironically, as an aside, that the wedding has taken place offstage: "Meanwhile he was a husband. Perhaps his union should have been emphasized before" (*LJ*, p. 181). That their marriage is one of good-fellowship rather than passion (*LJ*, pp. 181–82) is surely a pathetic irony, for Rickie has given up for Agnes a superior good-fellowship with Ansell and gets nothing in return. He does not even obtain a satisfactory Gerald-substitute, for "after all they never mentioned Gerald's name" (*LJ*, p. 182). Agnes and Rickie both know their marriage has failed; Agnes, who lacks imagination, is content, but Rickie is not. When Rickie blames his own "character" rather than marriage itself for the failure (*LJ*, p. 296), we don't quite believe him. He is right if we take his "character" to be his latent homosexuality, and he is right if we take his "character" to be his attraction to the negative values represented by Agnes and Gerald. But the feeling still remains that the novel itself, in the voice of Mrs. Failing, condemns marriage as an institution (*LJ*, p. 296). Only the fact that the novel ends with Stephen's happy marriage allows us to take Rickie at his word.

When the novel begins, Rickie is not interested in women and exhibits no desire to become so. He completely forgets that Agnes is coming to visit him, and when she appears, his first words to her are, "Agnes! Oh how perfectly awful!" (*LJ*, p. 5).[25] Rickie's reaction to his forgetfulness reflects

24. The novel's attitude toward Gerald reveals what Trilling, *Forster,* p. 17, calls Forster's "moral realism," his "respect for two facts co-existing": Forster despises Gerald but can invest his death "with a kind of primitive dignity."

25. Trilling, *Forster,* p. 77, sees this as significant: "Thus has his unconscious mind spoken for him, but he is unfortunately not to listen to his unconscious mind."

favorably on him, revealing humanity rather than chivalry: "he did not feel profoundly degraded, as a young man should who has acted discourteously to a young lady. Had he acted discourteously to his bedmaker or his gyp, he would have indeed minded just as much, which was not polite of him" (*LJ,* p. 6).

While not primarily physical, Rickie's relationship with Agnes can best be understood as a series of four physical embraces. The first embrace, by far the most important, unites Agnes and Gerald, with Rickie the awed onlooker. This embrace sets the tone for Rickie's later relationship with Agnes, for he remains an outsider even after Gerald's death (*LJ,* p. 64). During the second embrace, physically between Rickie and Agnes in the dell, Rickie thinks of Gerald; as Agnes kisses him, he cries, "Never forget that your greatest thing is over. . . . What he gave you then is greater than anything you will get from me" (*LJ,* p. 81). Agnes, frightened at this outburst, feels a "sense of something abnormal," probably Rickie's homosexuality, but she dismisses it as nonsense and kisses him. The homosexual aspect of Rickie's character is too strong to be overcome this easily by physical heterosexual love, however, largely because Rickie does not really accept physical sexuality at all. "Love, say orderly people, can be fallen into by two methods: (1) through the desires, (2) through the imagination" (*LJ,* p. 66); although the English consider the first method inferior, Forster asserts that those who use it "cannot breed a tragedy quite like Rickie's" (*LJ,* p. 66). Rickie accepts the physical side of his relationship with Agnes reluctantly (*LJ,* p. 71), thus dooming that relationship.

The third embrace connects their physical relationship with death, for they kiss on the train that kills a child at the level crossing, possibly at the exact moment of death (*LJ,* p. 103). The lack of a physical bridge over the railroad tracks here relates to the lack of a symbolic bridge at the time of the fourth embrace, when Agnes sees Stephen's brotherhood as dangerous and sexually prevents Rickie from acknowledging it, "stopping his advance quite frankly, with widespread arms" (*LJ*, p. 150). Here heterosexuality prevents brotherhood, specifically and dramatically demonstrating what Ansell has said in general terms; and Agnes further thwarts brotherhood by preventing Rickie from writing to Ansell about Stephen (*LJ*, p. 151). Later, Rickie's death is caused by a lack of both the physical and the symbolic bridge,[26] for Mrs. Failing fails to build the one, and Rickie, planning to go back to Agnes, loses his faith in the other, the bridge of brotherhood he has so tenuously established with an idealized Stephen.

Rickie is changed by Agnes as early as their engagement, and the changes are all negative. He views her as a "triumphant general, making each unit still more interesting. . . . He loved Agnes, not only for herself, but because she was lighting up the human world" (*LJ*, p. 117); but his perception is faulty; Agnes is connected only with artificial, electric light that has no warmth (*LJ*, pp. 193–94). Unlike Ansell, Agnes is the opposite of enlightening; because of his "new life" with her (*LJ*, p. 107), Rickie becomes *less* observant of the world, *less* sensitive to other people, and he does not pursue his potential relationship with Stephen:

Generally he was attracted by fresh people, and Stephen was almost fresh: they had been to him symbols of the unknown, and all that they did was interesting. But now he cared for the unknown no longer. He knew.

[*LJ*, p. 116]

Agnes thus twice stops Rickie from realizing his brotherhood with Stephen, both before and after they know of the physical kinship.

Before the revelation, Rickie assures Agnes that Mrs. Failing is "no more to us than the Wonham boy or the boot

26. Crews, *Perils of Humanism*, p. 64.

boy" (*LJ*, p. 136); but the theme of the novel is fraternity, and both Stephen and the boot boy are indeed his brothers. When Mrs. Failing reveals to Rickie his physical brotherhood with Stephen, Rickie denies it: "Stephen Wonham isn't my brother, Aunt Emily" (*LJ*, p. 142); the rest of the novel is spent finding out that he is, both factually and symbolically. Rickie must come to terms with his parents in order to accept Stephen's physical brotherhood, and he must come to terms with himself to accept him symbolically.

After Rickie knows, but before Agnes knows, she unintentionally prevents him once more from accepting his brotherhood (*LJ*, p. 143). When Rickie does tell Agnes that Stephen is his brother, it is at the level crossing where the child is killed (*LJ*, p. 143); and Stephen's concern for the child represents the brotherhood that Agnes, and Rickie, cannot accept. Not surprisingly, Stephen, who wants a bridge (*LJ*, p. 103), can easily accept his brotherhood when he finally does learn of it.

Rickie, because of Agnes, rejects the symbolic moment that could have saved him and does not tell Stephen "such a real thing" (*LJ*, p. 148). In rejecting Stephen, Rickie dooms himself; in accepting Agnes's condemnation of Stephen as "worse than a man diseased" (*LJ*, p. 151), he forgets that he himself is lame. As a result, he suffers a "curious breakdown" (*LJ*, p. 153), because

the heart of all things was hidden. There was a password and he could not learn it . . . had he not known the password once—known it and forgotten it already?

But at this point his fortunes become intimately connected with those of Mr. Pembroke.

[*LJ*, p. 158]

It is Rickie's brother-in-law who prevents him from rediscovering the password, "fratribus."

As a schoolteacher at a public school of the sort he despises, "Rickie's programme involved a change in values as

well as a change of occupation" (*LJ*, p. 167). He loses his independence to Herbert Pembroke (*LJ*, p. 178); his Cambridge friends grieve that "Pembroke and that wife simply
run him" (*LJ*, p. 195). Rickie is too complex a person to be
happy in the simplistic, inane, black-and-white world of
Herbert's school, for he suffers "from the Primal Curse,
which is not—as the Authorized Version suggests—the
knowledge of good and evil, but the knowledge of good-
and-evil," of the complexity of life (*LJ*, p. 186).

As he deteriorates, his marriage deteriorates with him,
but he does not realize that the lie about Stephen has
ruined their lives until he realizes that Agnes's attention to
Mrs. Failing amounts to legacy-hunting (*LJ*, p. 207). Rickie
begins to understand Agnes and becomes aware of how
greatly she has destroyed his freedom. He openly accuses
her of responsibility for Mrs. Failing's disowning Stephen
(*LJ*, p. 219), but when he tries to grab the letter that reveals
her guilt, everything from the dinner table falls on the
floor; Rickie is "swamped in domesticities" (*LJ*, p. 220) when
he attempts to make a moral stand about his brother. He
cannot defeat the domesticities, which include Herbert's intervention, and he apologizes to Agnes; but when he discovers that Stephen is the son of his mother, not his father,
he finally rejects both Agnes and Herbert and declares his
independence: "I never did belong to that great sect whose
doctrine is that each one should select—at least, I'm not
going to belong to it any longer" (*LJ*, p. 268).

Unfortunately, Rickie's acceptance of Stephen does not
really constitute an acceptance of brotherhood, for he
judges Stephen by their mother rather than by the man
himself; he goes to Stephen with their mother's portrait (*LJ*,
p. 272). Stephen offers Rickie real, personal, individual
brotherhood by attempting to show him the error of this
approach: "I simply came as I was, and I haven't altered
since" (*LJ*, p. 272). He tries to teach Rickie to react to people as people rather than as ideals:

Look me in the face. Don't hang on me clothes that don't belong—as you did on your wife, giving her saint's robes, whereas
she was simply a woman of her own sort, who needed careful
watching. Tear up the photographs.

[*LJ*, p. 287]

This is the most important lesson Rickie has to learn, but he
never learns it and dies in despair, reaccepting Sawston and
Failing values. He can save his brother but he cannot accept
him as real and thereby save himself. His deformity, his inability to walk with his brother, becomes complete as "the
train crushes both his legs." [27]

Stephen makes an accurate analysis of the basic flaw in
Rickie's relationship with Agnes—Rickie falls in love with a
goddess (*LJ*, p. 71), an empress (*LJ*, p. 18), a sibyl (*LJ*, p.
64), but not a woman—and relates this to Rickie's worship
of his mother. Rickie worships Agnes as Woman but is
never able to judge either her or Stephen clearly as people.[28]

Ironically, although Rickie sees Agnes as Woman, Agnes
herself wishes she were a man: "The whole world lies before them. They can do anything. They aren't cooped up
with servants and teaparties and twaddle" (*LJ*, p. 79). While
we do not like Agnes personally, we must sympathize with
her plight as a woman, as we did with Lilia's in *Where Angels
Fear to Tread*. Agnes is a good housekeeper, always woman's
primary job; but for a member of Agnes's social class,
"keeping house" essentially means merely supervising servants, a job which provides no outlet for her energies. Like
Mrs. Herriton in *Where Angels Fear to Tread*, Agnes diverts
her unused energies into indirect, destructive manipulation.
When she seduces Rickie into the dell, she does it passively:
"I thought you would never come to me" (*LJ*, p. 80); as a
woman, she cannot go to him. When Agnes is congratulated

27. Alan Wilde, *Art and Order: A Study of E. M. Forster* (New York: New York University Press, 1964), p. 40.
28. Edgerton, "The Androgynous Mind," p. 52, calls the Person "Homo," as opposed to "Woman" or "Man."

on her engagement to Rickie, it is "a social blunder" (*LJ*, p. 90), for no one is supposed to admit that the woman may have caught the man. However, this backwards congratulation occurs twice in Forster, here and in *A Room with a View,* and confirms the fact that this is precisely what everyone does think. Although Agnes complains about the inequities of her position as a woman, she is not above using the unfair "privileges" of her femininity; personally not very bright, she gets around difficult questions of philosophy and religion by taking advantage of the fact that women are not expected to think for themselves (*LJ*, p. 113). She is conventionally unconventional; her "emancipation," like everything else about her, is opportunistic.

Agnes's narrowness and philistinism are presented to us early in the novel, ironically expressed in pseudobiblical prose: "she cared not what men might do unto her, for she had her own splendid lover, who could have knocked all these unhealthy undergraduates into a cocked-hat" (*LJ*, p. 7). Her happiness is at the expense of others, a fact which places her squarely in the ranks of anti-intellectual conventionality. Not surprisingly, her intolerance of the different and the "abnormal" makes her hate Rickie after Gerald's death: " 'These are the people who are left alive!' From the bottom of her soul she hated him" (*LJ*, p. 57). Agnes never really stops hating Rickie; she always resents the fact that he is alive and Gerald dead; so she destroys him, or at least that part of him which Gerald never had, the spiritual part. Yet we must give her credit for recognizing Rickie's greatness when he tells her to mind Gerald's death.[29] Forster asserts the "tragedy" of Agnes's fate; he does not like her, but he is scrupulously fair to her:

Agnes also has her tragedy. She belonged to the type—not necessarily an elevated one—that loves once and once only. Her love

29. Trilling, *Forster,* pp. 16–17, calls this Forster's "double turn": "after Gerald's death he can give Agnes Pembroke her moment of tragic nobility, only to pursue her implacably for her genteel brutality."

for Gerald had not been a noble passion: no imagination transfigured it. But such as it was, it sprang to embrace him, and he carried it away with him when he died. . . . She is not conscious of her tragedy, and therefore only the gods need weep at it. But it is fair to remember that hitherto she moves as one from whom the inner life has been withdrawn.

[*LJ*, pp. 215–16]

We must pity Agnes because her lover is dead and her Life Force destroyed, but we must also judge her by the person that lover was—a brutal, stupid bully.

For Agnes, as for Caroline Abbott in *Where Angels Fear to Tread*, "The greatest thing is over" (*LJ*, p. 58). Caroline realizes this herself, however, while Agnes must be told: Rickie cries, "his arms will never hold you again" (*LJ*, p. 57) as he implores her to appreciate Gerald's *physical* absence. Agnes will never again achieve sexual transcendence. Her loss is primarily physical (she certainly can't miss Gerald's mind), but she never realizes this, and when she reacts honestly for once, when she reacts sexually to a Stephen who reminds her physically of Gerald, she is horrified and hates him for it (*LJ*, p. 279). In the end Agnes is vindictive; she blames her suffering on men whom she has harmed much more than they have harmed her (*LJ*, p. 278), and we do not forgive her.

At the moment Agnes minds Gerald's death, she blames Herbert for postponing her marriage (*LJ*, p. 58). Herbert plays an important role in this novel, that of negative example; he is stupid and anti-intellectual, frigid and antisexual. His attitude toward life, and toward "engagements" particularly, is in direct opposition to Ansell's view. Ansell asserts early in the novel that "The only real reason for doing a thing is because you want to do it. . . . the talk about 'engagements' is cant" (*LJ*, p. 34). Although he is referring specifically to the sort of engagement that forces one to visit someone else out of a sense of duty, he could well be speaking of marital engagements, too, and we readily accept his view over Herbert's. Herbert believes in the practical suppression of passion and is directly responsible for the "long engagement" (*LJ*, p. 37) which dooms Agnes and Gerald and prevents them from consummating their love. One would expect Herbert to learn a lesson from Gerald's death, but he does not and neither does Agnes, for they plan another long engagement, between Agnes and Rickie (*LJ*, pp. 84; 91).

Agnes and Rickie marry as soon as they do only because of Herbert's selfishness, for he wants to use Agnes as housekeeper to further his own advancement at Sawston School (*LJ*, p. 163). The school itself, the horrible outcome of a spirit like Herbert's, is a ghastly parody of Cambridge. Rickie reaches his lowest point when he accedes to Herbert and participates in the public school system, a system Forster hates and from which he derives his theme of "the undeveloped heart." [30] Herbert is the prime example of an undeveloped heart in *The Longest Journey*, and his own attempt at marriage is as pathetic as it is ironic. After being violently refused by the first woman he asks, Herbert considers marrying a "Miss Herriton" (*LJ*, p. 163), a fitting choice, for in *Where Angels Fear to Tread* Harriet Herriton is the embodiment of the narrow rigidity of Sawston. Like the Herritons, the Pembrokes lead a home life characterized by power politics: Agnes "gained her brother as an ally" against Stephen (*LJ*, p. 222). Herbert's influence is such that after the marriage between Rickie and Agnes, we think of all three of them as "the Pembrokes," and in fact Agnes seems closer to Herbert than she ever does to Rickie (*LJ*, p. 223). However, their relationship is quite different and far inferior to the sisterhood between Helen and Margaret Schlegel in *Howards End*.

The home life of Mr. and Mrs. Elliot when Rickie was a child was as awful as his life with the Pembrokes after he is married. Rickie "was never told anything, but he discovered

30. Ibid., pp. 27–28.

for himself that his father and mother did not love each other, and that his mother was lovable" (*LJ*, p. 25). His father is a terrible man who forces his family to live in a suburb similar to Sawston (*LJ*, p. 23) and sends his son to a public school, similar to Sawston School, that he hates (*LJ*, p. 26). Mr. Elliot condescends to and laughs at both his son and his wife; the hatred he inspires in Rickie evokes a compensatory worship of his mother, a sweet, gentle woman whose one act of rebellion gives the novel's plot its pivot.

Mrs. Elliot's plight as wife is representative of what can happen to a woman trapped in an unhappy marriage:

> She had to manage the servants, to hush the neighbouring children, to answer the correspondence, to paper and re-paper the rooms—and all for the sake of a man whom she did not like, and who did not conceal his dislike for her.
>
> [*LJ*, p. 27]

She is much happier after her husband's death (*LJ*, p. 28), but she survives him by only eleven days (*LJ*, p. 30). She exists only to suffer, to be her husband's slave; as a woman, she is not allowed to live for herself.[31] Like Mrs. Herriton, Mrs. Elliot has no first name and no maiden name; she exists only as wife—particularly the wife of an evil man— and as mother. That she embodies woman's two traditional roles leaves her open to the charge of unreality: as "just" a wife and mother, she exists only in people's reactions to her, as women are expected to live.[32] Mrs. Elliot is particularly unfortunate in the people who react to her, for Mr. Elliot is nasty and judges her only on taste, Rickie is lonely and idol-

31. Trilling, ibid., p. 47, seems unfair when he asserts that "Rickie Elliot's mother, although very tender, was late in coming to love her son and never seems wholly attached to him"; he here does not take into account the central point of the novel, that *no one* should have to be "wholly attached" to anyone.

32. We must ask if all women are unreal, as Ansell implies, or if only good women are unreal, as Trilling, ibid., p. 115, suggests: "Agnes and Mrs. Failing are entirely alive, but Rickie's mother, the symbol of life, is dead and a spirit." Trilling's dichotomy resolves itself when we view Mrs. Elliot not as the symbol of life but as the symbol of *woman's* life.

izes her, and Stephen is not allowed, by society, to know her; only Robert reacts to her as to another "person." Although she does break away from society's conventional mold in her love affair with Robert, she cannot stay away, and her life ends with that of her husband.

Mrs. Elliot is virtually driven into her love affair with Robert; she resists as long as she can, but Mr. Elliot has one unforgivable fault:

He did not like her, he practically lived apart, he was not even faithful or polite. These were grave faults, but they were human ones: she could even imagine them in a man she loved. What she could never love was a dilettante.

[*LJ*, p. 252]

He sees life as a comedy; having no idea that life is real, he refuses to take seriously his wife's plea to "save" her from what she sees as infidelity (*LJ*, p. 254). Robert, if anyone, is the savior, for Robert has Ansell's view of "engagements" rather than the conventional one: "if Mrs. Elliot was happier than he could ever make her, he would withdraw, and love her in renunciation. But if he could make her happier, he would love her in fulfilment" (*LJ*, p. 251). However, no permanent salvation is possible in this novel, and Robert's sexual rescue of Mrs. Elliot is only temporary. After a blissful seventeen days in Sweden, Robert drowns and Mrs. Elliot makes Agnes's mistake:

When her lover sank, eluding her last embrace, she thought, as Agnes was to think after her, that her soul had sunk with him, and that never again should she be capable of earthly love.

[*LJ*, p. 257]

But Mrs. Elliot soon realizes that this is wrong:

Stephen was born, and altered her life. She could still love people passionately; she still drew strength from the heroic past. . . .

And a curious thing happened. Her second child drew her towards her first.

[*LJ*, pp. 257–58]

She must pay a price for flouting and then returning to
convention: "to keep her bond, she must see this son only as
a stranger" (*LJ*, p. 257), and Stephen knows her only as
"Mrs. Elliot, a pleasant woman" (*LJ*, p. 259). Unlike Agnes,
the first Mrs. Elliot in the novel is both honest and fair;
realizing that she is "protected by the conventions," she is
willing to "pay them their fee" (*LJ*, p. 258).

Mrs. Failing, although primarily an extension of Rickie's
father, supports Rickie's mother in her flight from convention and does not demand that she pay any fee: to Mrs.
Failing, Mrs. Elliot and Robert are "guiltless in the sight of
God" (*LJ*, p. 255). Mrs. Failing changes in the course of her
life more than any other character in the novel. Her support of Mrs. Elliot comes when she is young: "The world
was not so humorous then, but it had been more important"
(*LJ*, p. 99). When young, she hates Rickie's father (*LJ*, p.
100), but as she ages, she resembles him more and more,
seeing life as only a comedy. She is "essentially an androgynous figure; even her perversity is shared by Rickie's
father." [33] Mrs. Failing does object to being called "she" in
front of the servants (*LJ*, p. 98), and she feels no identification with other women: in church she has only contempt for
the "poor women, with flat, hopeless faces" whom she sees
"Sunday after Sunday, but did not know their names" (*LJ*,
p. 134). If she is indeed androgynous, she represents all
that is bad and unloving in both sexes, not what is good.

We identify Mrs. Failing with Agnes as much as we do
with Mr. Elliot. Like Agnes, she is conventionally unconventional and manipulative; [34] like Agnes, she marries a

33. George H. Thomson, *The Fiction of E. M. Forster* (Detroit, Wayne University Press, 1967), p. 148.
34. Frederick P. W. McDowell, *E. M. Forster* (New York, Twayne Publishers,
1969), p. 79.

man who is weaker than she, a man whom she does not love and whom she helps destroy. Her marriage, like Agnes and Rickie's and like Mr. and Mrs. Elliot's, is a failure; and when Emily Elliot marries a man named "Failing," she contributes much to bringing about his failure, as do Agnes and Mr. Elliot, less allegorically, with their mates. Mrs. Failing, "unconventional" herself, tries to convince Rickie to rely on the same conventions she rejects, to go back to Agnes. In the end she believes that "the important things in life are little things," not people (*LJ*, p. 295); and Rickie, unfortunately, believes her. He should not, for Mrs. Failing is discredited in our eyes in three ways: (1) by her identification with Agnes; (2) by her identification with Mr. Elliot; and most importantly, (3) by her disdain and fear of the earth itself (*LJ*, pp. 294–95).

It is Mrs. Failing, however, who reveals Stephen, the natural man, to be Rickie's brother. Like all the Elliots, she cannot accept brotherhood herself: she will not bridge the railroad crossing; but the Elliot deformity, her lameness, becomes most painful when a child is killed there (*LJ*, p. 98). When she does tell Rickie that Stephen is his brother, she does so out of malice, and the final judgment of her is harsh:

she had forgotten what people were like. Finding life dull, she had dropped lies into it. . . . She loved to mislead others, and in the end her private view of false and true was obscured, and she misled herself. How she must have enjoyed their errors over Stephen! But her own error had been greater, inasmuch as it was spiritual entirely.

[*LJ*, p. 297]

Stephen represents the hope for the future at the end of the book. "When Stephen persuades Rickie to desert Agnes he performs the identical service that his father did for Mrs. Elliot. He intrudes the wisdom of nature into a custom-ridden marriage." [35] Stephen cannot give Rickie a child di-

35. Crews, *Perils of Humanism*, p. 60.

rectly, as his father did their mother, but Stephen does have his own child at the end of the novel and names her after his and Rickie's mother, thus giving Rickie the only physical posterity he gets:

[Rickie's] spirit had fled, in agony and loneliness, never to know that it bequeathed him salvation. . . . One thing remained that a man of his sort might do. He bent down reverently and saluted the child; to whom he had given the name of their mother.

[*LJ*, p. 311]

We never know what that name is, and physical posterity, while important, is not the most important thing. Rickie's own child dies, but after Rickie's death Agnes has another child, and we are surely not supposed to believe that her posterity is in any way superior to his because more direct. The spiritual posterity that Rickie leaves Stephen certainly transcends the physical.

Stephen is the primary representative of heterosexuality in the novel, with Ansell representing homosexuality and Rickie, confused, somewhere in between.[36] Agnes cannot accept Stephen in the role of brother, for women in this novel cannot accept fraternity, but she can react to him sexually. Agnes's heterosexuality is destructive, while Stephen's is not; he does not "use" women, for "That would be harming some one else" (*LJ*, p. 284), a highly moral position which Henry Wilcox in *Howards End* does not understand. *The Longest Journey* offers Rickie a double fraternity including both Ansell and Stephen, homo- and heterosexual love, but Rickie cannot accept both any more than he can accept either, for he cannot see people as real. Stephen is identified with Ansell's image, the match, as Stephen and Rickie watch the burning paper on the river (*LJ*, p. 293). The paper vanishes for Rickie but will burn forever for Stephen.

Stephen is "utterly committed to Demeter's spirit."[37]

36. Ibid., p. 136.   37. Ibid.

When we first meet him, his room holds "only one picture—the Demeter of Cnidos" (*LJ*, p. 129), and after Rickie's death he adds the picture of Stockholm; both pictures connect him with his mother, whom we may see as Demeter.[38] Forster's 1904 essay "Cnidus" suggests an androgynous Demeter:

Demeter alone among gods has true immortality. . . . to her, all over the world, rise prayers of idolatry from suffering men as well as suffering women, for she has transcended sex.[39]

If Mrs. Elliot is indeed androgynous, our view of her as symbolic of woman's plight becomes even more relevant. Representing all that is good and loving in both sexes, she effectively extends the metaphor of suffering and oppressed woman to include suffering man, the gentle and sensitive outsider in whom Forster is most interested and about whom he writes in all of his books, regardless of the actual physical sex of the protagonists.

38. Thomson, *Fiction*, p. 144.
39. E. M. Forster, "Cnidus," in *Abinger Harvest*, p. 176.

Three
A Room with a View

A Room with a View, a "problem" novel, deals with two problems: (1) the acceptance of sexuality and the life of the body, and (2) sexual equality and the role of women in society. Like all problem novels, it is somewhat dated, but the extent to which it is not dated is rather remarkable, rather depressing, and indeed rather recent: A Room with a View was more dated seven years ago than it is today. In 1967 Professor Herbert Howarth, lecturing to a graduate literature class at the University of Pennsylvania, suggested that the main problem with Forster's novels was that most of his problems had already been solved.[1] He cited specifically the problem of the emancipation of women in A Room with a View and Howards End; at the time the assertion seemed accurate. Seven years later, in 1974, the problem of the role of women in society seems at least as controversial as it did in 1908 and considerably more so than it did in 1967. In addition, Maurice has been published, and the problem of the homosexual and his role in society, also a problem crucially relevant today, has been added to the list of Forster's themes. Only regarding the acceptance of sexuality can we still agree with Mr. Howarth's assertion: in that area society appears to have made some progress.

A condensed and revised version of this chapter appeared under the title "Forster's Women: A Room with a View" in English Literature in Transition, 1880–1920, Vol. 16, No. 4 (1973).
1. Howarth, Nov. 1, 1967.

The theme of the acceptance of sexuality is integrally connected with the structure of *A Room with a View,* which hinges on three kisses. The first kiss is spontaneous, natural, and beautiful: George Emerson, taken by surprise, kisses an equally startled Lucy Honeychurch in a field of violets. The aftermath of this kiss defines the role of Lucy's cousin and chaperone, Charlotte, "who stood brown against the view." [2] George's first kiss is contrasted to Cecil's kiss, which is a failure; Cecil, Lucy's fiancé, is a prude and asks permission for something Forster believes *should* be spontaneous and natural:

Passion should believe itself irresistible. It should forget civility and consideration and all the other curses of a refined nature. Above all, it should never ask for leave where there is a right of way.

[*R,* p. 124]

The last of the three kisses is again George's and is again spontaneous and natural, for unlike Cecil, George "loved passionately" (*R,* p. 187). George is obviously Lucy's proper mate, a fact it takes her the entire length of the novel to realize, for she is not a person of extraordinary insight and has been taught to suppress passion. Her growing ability to trust her own feelings and intuitions rather than "propriety" provides the central action of the book.

Lucy's first act of rebellion is to buy a picture of Botticelli's "Birth of Venus," although Charlotte attempts to dissuade her from buying it because "Venus, being a pity, spoilt the picture, otherwise so charming . . . (A pity in art of course signified the nude)" (*R,* p. 47). Later, the sight of George's naked body helps Lucy in her development. His body is beautiful, and Forster presents the sight of a naked human body as a force against muddle, a force which con-

2. E. M. Forster, *A Room with a View* (New York, Vintage paperback, 1966), p. 80. All future references to this work will follow the pagination of this readily available edition and will appear in the text in the abbreviated form *R*.

vention attempts to stifle.[3] Lucy, influenced by Charlotte and the forces of propriety, has tried to avoid George after their first kiss and is surprised by her second meeting with him. He has been bathing in the "Sacred Lake" with her brother, Freddy, and Mr. Beebe, the clergyman, and is first undressed and then half-dressed: "Who could foretell that she and George would meet in the rout of a civilization, amidst an army of coats and collars and boots that lay wounded over the sunlit earth?" (*R*, p. 154). At the sight of George, both Lucy and her mother attempt "the tense yet nonchalant expression that is suitable for ladies on such occasions" (*R*, p. 152). But Mrs. Honeychurch, a realistic, humorous person, "found it impossible to remain shocked" (*R*, p. 153). Lucy's first reaction is to attempt to be proper: she "was all parasol and evidently 'minded' " (*R*, p. 152), but afterwards "her defences fell, and she entertained an image that had physical beauty" (*R*, p. 165). By appearing before her naked, George exposes Lucy to an important aspect of life and of freedom that is ordinarily denied her as a woman.

The freedom of men to bathe naked, which Forster contrasts with the lack of freedom for women to do the same thing (*R*, p. 123), points out the second central theme of *A Room with a View*, the question of the freedom of women in society. A little thing like bathing is considered unladylike, and Forster shows the demands of being "ladylike" to be extremely and pointlessly constricting. Quite early in the novel Lucy plaintively asks, "Why were most big things unladylike?" (*R*, p. 46), and as the novel progresses, she finds Charlotte's answer increasingly unsatisfactory:

It was not that ladies were inferior to men; it was that they were different. Their mission was to inspire others to achievement rather than to achieve themselves. Indirectly, by means of tact and a spotless name, a lady could accomplish much. But if she rushed

3. Howarth, Nov. 8, 1967.

into the fray herself she would be first censured, then despised, and finally ignored. Poems had been written to illustrate this point.

[*R*, p. 46]

A Room with a View is a poem written to illustrate the opposite point. The ideal to which Lucy is taught to aspire is that of the "mediaeval lady," and Forster explicitly contrasts the quality of life allowed "mediaeval" women to that offered to men: "Men, declaring that she inspires them to it, move joyfully over the surface, having the most delightful meetings with other men, happy, not because they are masculine, but because they are alive" (*R*, p. 47). Forster recognizes that women are not allowed to live full lives, that "masculine" does not equal "alive" but is rather, in this society, a necessary precondition to it. The male narrative voice effects a hugely successful irony when it realizes that chivalry is now a part-time affair: "It is sweet to protect her in the intervals of business, sweet to pay her honour when she has cooked our dinner well" (*R*, p. 47). Obviously, no dragons are left; a woman's role is no longer maiden-in-distress but consists of cooking dinner, or playing servant. Forster purposefully overwrites the entire section dealing with the medieval lady in order to show the legend's absurdity, and he recognizes the constrictions of such an ideal in an interesting, vibrant world: "Before the show breaks up she would like to drop the august title of the Eternal Woman, and go there as her transitory self" (*R*, p. 47). In Forster's world, transitory selfness is the only kind there is, and by denying it to women, by forcing them into the chivalric, medieval, "eternal" mold, society destroys their individuality and their ability to live unique, whole, participatory lives. Forster strongly implies that if women are not allowed off their pedestals, the show will indeed break up.

Lucy's rebellion from the medieval mold is given form by her experience in Italy:

A rebel she was, but not of the kind [Cecil] understood—a rebel who desired, not a wider dwelling-room, but equality beside the man she loved. For Italy was offering her the most priceless of all possessions—her own soul.

[*R*, p. 128]

Italy itself cannot offer Lucy freedom, for Italy does not give equality to its own women, as Forster points out in *Where Angels Fear to Tread*. But the experience of Italy expands Lucy's sensitivity enough for her to see, eventually, that her future lies with George, who does offer her equality. Forster speaks of "the eternal league of Italy with youth" (*R*, p. 61), and their relationship appropriately begins there. Italy and Italians represent the natural world: "In the company of this common man the world was beautiful and direct. For the first time she felt the influence of Spring" (*R*, p. 79). The driver and his girlfriend are Phaethon and Persephone (*R*, p. 68), and Phaethon's interpretation of "good men" (*R*, p. 78), the closest Lucy can get to "clergymen" in Italian, takes her instead to George so that they might kiss. Lucy and George are parallel to the Italian lovers: Mr. Eager catches Phaethon and Persephone kissing and disapproves, as Charlotte catches and disapproves of Lucy and George. Old Mr. Emerson, George's father, supports Phaethon and Persephone in their love; he will later support George and Lucy in theirs.

The British world of the Pension Bertolini is contrasted with the Italian world of nature. Among the older English people, only Mr. Emerson emerges on the side of nature; the others are totally hemmed in by arbitrary roles, by what is considered "ladylike" or its converse, "manly." Even when they barely escape death during a storm, they are embarrassed by their human and spontaneous show of feeling: "The older people recovered quickly. In the very height of their emotion they knew it to be unmanly or unladylike" (*R*, p. 84). The storm they cannot react to naturally seems the

direct outcome of Charlotte's "brown" interruption of Lucy
and George's natural kiss, and reveals the English world to
be inadequate and frigid.

The Pension Bertolini itself represents the British world
in miniature and includes all the necessary types: Mr.
Beebe, the clergyman; Miss Lavish, the "intellectual"; Lucy,
the young girl, and Charlotte, the chaperone; Mr. Emerson,
the free thinker, and George, the young man; and of course
"the Miss Alans, who stood for good breeding" (*R*, p. 43).
The Miss Alans represent the social force of early Victorian
propriety and prudery (*R*, p. 42). Their attitude toward sex
and the body is directly opposite that of Mr. Emerson, and
they are quite shocked when he uses the word "stomach" in
mixed company (*R*, p. 41). An amusing touch in an amusing book, near the end of the novel they present a real
threat: Lucy almost rejects George to embrace Miss Alandom. She is saved from that funny but pathetic fate only
because of Mr. Emerson.

Mr. Emerson is the most clearly positive character; he is
the foremost spokesman for both equality between the sexes
and acceptance of the life of the body. When we are introduced to him at the Pension Bertolini he is described as
"one of the ill-bred people whom one does meet abroad"
(*R*, p. 4). He dares to talk to Lucy and Charlotte without
waiting for a proper introduction, and he offers them his
view, a kindly and symbolic gesture, for his view ultimately
does prevail. He asserts that "Women like looking at a view;
men don't" (*R*, p. 5); but this dichotomy between men and
women is not arbitrary, like Ansell's in *The Longest Journey*.
Mr. Emerson's belief in sexual equality does not blind him
to the fact that the sexes are indeed different, that they like
and mind different things. The chief difference between his
view and Ansell's is that Ansell ascribes the differences he
perceives to an implacable Nature, while Mr. Emerson attributes them to a difference in upbringing, a more sympathetic approach. Although Mr. Emerson mistrusts propriety

itself, he feels personally concerned about individual representatives of it and is distressed at incommoding the Miss
Alans, for "Women mind such a thing" (*R*, p. 176).

Mr. Emerson's view of life is affirmative: he believes that
"by the side of the everlasting Why there is a Yes—a transitory Yes if you like, but a Yes" (*R*, p. 32). He rejects traditional religion, yet he is "profoundly religious, and differed
from Mr. Beebe chiefly by his acknowledgement of passion"
(*R*, p. 234). He uses religious metaphor and predicts that
the Garden of Eden will come only when men and women
achieve equality, when both accept their bodies and their
sexuality: "In this—not in other things—we men are
ahead. We despise the body less than women do. But not
until we are comrades shall we enter the garden" (*R*, p.
146). He teaches that "love is of the body; not the body, but
of the body" (*R*, p. 237), that directness is necessary "to lib-
erate the soul" (*R*, p. 237). His directness liberates Lucy's
soul: Mr. Emerson realizes that Lucy loves George and tells
her that she must marry him or waste her life (*R*, p. 237).
His face revives her from despair: "It was the face of a saint
who understood" (*R*, p. 239). Asserting that "we fight for
more than Love or Pleasure; there is Truth. Truth counts,
Truth does count" (*R*, p. 240), Mr. Emerson gives Lucy the
strength to trust herself. "He had robbed the body of its
taint, the world's taunts of their sting; he had shown her the
holiness of direct desire" (*R*, p. 240). Because of him, Lucy
and George also are able to partake of the transitory Yes.

Miss Eleanor Lavish is Mr. Emerson's obverse: everything
genuinely unconventional about him is falsely "original"
about her; her name hardly needs comment. That "Miss
Lavish is so original" is "the supreme achievement of the
Pension Bertolini in the way of definition" (*R*, pp. 37–38).
But both Lucy (*R*, p. 23) and Mr. Beebe (*R*, p. 38) come to
doubt its validity. Ironically, the narrow world of the Pension accepts in Miss Lavish what it rejects in Mr. Emerson,
perhaps because her hypocrisy poses no real threat to its

own.[4] Whereas Mr. Emerson desires only to help people, and is always surprised when their reaction is shock, Miss Lavish shocks people for the sake of shocking them. Mr. Emerson cares about people, while Miss Lavish cares only about the impression she makes on them. Her desire to see "the true Italy" (*R*, p. 19) rather than to see Italians reveals her as superficial, as will Adela Quested's desire to see "the real India" in *A Passage to India*. Miss Lavish's definition of "true democracy" as "a little civility to your inferiors" (*R*, p. 20) shows her to be a snob.

Charlotte Bartlett admires her extraordinarily as "a really clever woman" (*R*, p. 58), and their friendship unites the worst kind of propriety with the worst kind of emancipation. Charlotte sees Eleanor as "emancipated, but only in the very best sense of the word. . . . She believes in justice and truth and human interest. . . . she has a high opinion of the destiny of woman—" (*R*, p. 58); Miss Lavish's belief in "human interest" does not stand up to Mr. Emerson's belief in humanity, and even her feminism is false, for she takes the pen name of a man (*R*, p. 183); Mr. Emerson is a truer exponent of the rights of women than she. Her novel's description of the kiss between Lucy and George only perpetuates arbitrary and conventional sexual roles: "There came from his lips no wordy protestation such as formal lovers use. No eloquence was his, nor did he suffer from the lack of it. He simply enfolded her in his manly arms" (*R*, p. 186).[5]

Charlotte Bartlett, Lucy's prim cousin and chaperone, is a much more complex character. Miss Bartlett, Miss Lavish, and the two Miss Alans represent all the options open to celibate women. At first, Miss Bartlett seems merely a younger and poorer version of the Miss Alans, but she ul-

4. Wilde, *Art and Order*, p. 52, sees her as "a rather pathetic maiden lady, . . . unwilling to look squarely at the not always pleasant truth about herself and the world around her."

5. Crews, *Perils of Humanism*, p. 87, accurately describes this as "a fidgety romanticism."

timately exemplifies "Forster's insistence on the double turn, on the something else that lies behind." [6] Charlotte inhibits Lucy at the beginning, but at the end she effects Lucy's union with George by setting up her interview with Mr. Emerson. Although the novel does very subtly lay the groundwork for Charlotte's change of heart, the effect remains one of surprise and of gratitude that she is not totally at the mercy of the frigid propriety she seems to represent.

Before we are aware of her "other side," Miss Bartlett seems to embody the "petty unselfishness" Caroline Abbott so deplores in *Where Angels Fear to Tread;* indeed, Charlotte seems virtually impossible to live with: "Unselfishness with Miss Bartlett had entirely usurped the functions of enthusiasm" (*R*, p. 77). Her unselfishness is manipulative, and she gets what she wants by inducing guilt in others: when she, Miss Lavish, and Lucy must share only two mackintosh squares, she drives Lucy away by sitting down "where the ground looked particularly moist" (*R*, p. 77). Her primary characteristic is making other people uncomfortable, and her favorite role is "that of the prematurely aged martyr" (*R*, p. 91).

Charlotte is absurdly prudish about sex and the body; her reason for giving Lucy the smaller of the two Emerson rooms, that it belonged to old Mr. Emerson rather than "the young man," bewilders us as much as it bewilders Lucy (*R*, p. 15). When George casually announces that his father is in the bath, Miss Bartlett and the Miss Alan to whom she is speaking at the time are shocked: " 'Oh, dear!' breathed the little old lady, and shuddered as if all the winds of heaven had entered the apartment. 'Gentlemen sometimes do not realize—' Her voice faded away, but Miss Bartlett seemed to understand and a conversation developed, in which gentlemen who did not thoroughly realize played a principal part. Lucy, not realizing either, was reduced to literature" (*R*, p. 14). To Charlotte, beauty and delicacy are

6. Trilling, *Forster*, p. 16.

the same thing (*R,* p. 13), and men are the enemy (*R,* p. 88).

Her reaction to George's kissing Lucy reveals the dirty mind of the prude: she is concerned only with silencing him, because she is convinced that men of his "type" "seldom keep their exploits to themselves" (*R,* p. 87); Lucy winces at "the horrible plural" (*R,* p. 87). Charlotte bases her condemnation of George on his comment that "liking one person is an extra reason for liking another" (*R,* p. 87), a theory which hardly calls for the term "exploits." Indeed, it is the theme of *The Longest Journey,* and it is reconciled in *A Room with a View* with heterosexual monogamy. Charlotte asks Lucy, "When he insulted you, how would you have replied?" (*R,* p. 88), but Lucy does not know how she would have replied, for she is not given a chance to form her own opinion; she is merely told that "kiss" equals "insult." Charlotte is horrified at the thought of what might have happened if she had not arrived at the scene of the crime, but we feel that without the force of "brown" society, which tries to thwart natural, spontaneous feeling, Lucy would have been able to react to George's kiss spontaneously and personally instead of "properly."

Charlotte yearns for the return of chivalry, for "a real man" (*R,* p. 89) to defend Lucy's honor; but the whole "problem" has arisen because George is a real man and not a fake knight. Charlotte's desire for "some men who can reverence woman" (*R,* p. 89) harks back to the ideal of the medieval lady, and reverencing woman here precludes loving *a* woman. Charlotte functions as a negative example of brown society:

She had worked like a great artist; for a time—indeed, for years— she had been meaningless, but at the end there was presented to the girl the complete picture of a cheerless, loveless world in which the young rush to destruction until they learn better—a shamefaced world of precautions and barriers which may avert evil, but which do not seem to bring good, if we may judge from those who have used them most.

[*R,* pp. 92–93]

But at the end, there is that double turn to explain, and the only satisfactory explanation is that Charlotte has wanted Lucy and George to get together all along. George's final analysis, that "She is not frozen, Lucy, she is not withered up all through" (*R*, p. 246), gives the novel an optimistic ending, for if there is hope for Charlotte, there is hope for almost everyone.

There is surely hope for Lucy, whose very name implies light as opposed to darkness and muddle.[7] She is intuitive rather than intelligent, "slow to follow what people said, but quick enough to detect what they meant" (*R*, p. 113); in this, she anticipates Maurice. Early in the book, Lucy becomes aware of the deeper implications of the Emersons and their room with a view:

she had an odd feeling that whenever these ill-bred tourists spoke the contest widened and deepened till it dealt, not with rooms and views, but with—well, with something quite different, whose existence she had not realized before.

[*R*, p. 6]

Lucy's natural inclination is to be nice to the Emersons (*R*, p. 8), and her intuition is accurate, for the Emersons represent freedom and the sanctity of personal relations. When George first addresses Lucy he questions the rules of propriety that determine what a lone female may and may not do (*R*, p. 26). When propriety then tells Lucy to be demure, to be offended at George "or at all events be offended before him" (*R*, pp. 26–27), it is demanding "connection" on false, impersonal grounds. Conventional sex roles demand such a reaction to "a young man" regardless of the specific individual or situation involved, but the Emerson "view" is precisely the opposite. When Lucy becomes so entranced by the Emersons "that she could not remember how to behave" (*R*, p. 27), she takes her first step toward accepting their view that people are not supposed to behave according to arbitrary, prescribed rules.

7. Howarth, Nov. 8, 1967.

Lucy's last name, "Honeychurch," introduces the anticlerical tone of the novel, but her first reaction to Mr. Beebe is one of welcome. Indeed, Lucy likes Mr. Beebe so much that she says, "No one would take him for a clergyman" (*R*, p. 11), and she sees him as a relief from Charlotte. This sets up the central irony of the novel, for at the end Charlotte and Mr. Beebe change places, and Charlotte is revealed to be in favor of life, Mr. Beebe against it. Early in the novel, however, Mr. Beebe seems a very attractive character. He exhibits "tolerance, sympathy, and a sense of humour" (*R*, p. 40); he approves of the Emersons (*R*, p. 10); and his pictures of Lucy in Italy are quite apt: "Miss Honeychurch as a kite, Miss Bartlett holding the string. Picture number two: the string breaks" (*R*, p. 106).

Three forces encourage the string to break: Italy, George, and music. Italy is the sky in which the kite first flies, George the wind which puts tension on the string, and music the internal makeup of the kite itself which allows it to respond to the wind. The string does not actually break, however; Charlotte lets go.

Music is what makes Lucy special; it is her one "illogical element" (*R*, p. 35), and without it she is rather ordinary. Like Maurice's homosexuality, Lucy's music does not lead directly to salvation but rather prepares her for it. Her music ultimately allows her to "connect," as Mr. Beebe predicts:

Does it seem reasonable that she should play so wonderfully, and live so quietly? I suspect that one day she will be wonderful in both. The water-tight compartments in her will break down, and music and life will mingle. Then we shall have her heroically good, heroically bad—too heroic, perhaps, to be good or bad.

[*R*, p. 106]

Her awareness of touch when she plays the piano leads to her acceptance of that other touch, sexuality: "Like every true performer, she was intoxicated by the mere feel of the notes: they were fingers caressing her own; and by touch, not by sound alone, did she come to her desire" (*R*, p. 35). Her music takes her beyond propriety and freedom; when playing the piano, she is "no longer either deferential or patronizing; no longer either a rebel or a slave" (*R*, p. 34). She first becomes conscious of her discontent after playing the piano (*R*, p. 48), and that discontent leads her directly into George's arms.

Wishing that something would happen to her, Lucy enters the Piazza Signoria and discovers sexuality in the image of a tower: [8]

> She fixed her eyes wistfully on the tower of the palace, which rose out of the lower darkness like a pillar of roughened gold. It seemed no longer a tower, no longer supported by earth, but some unattainable treasure throbbing in the tranquil sky. . . .
> Then something did happen.
>
> [*R*, p. 48]

A man is stabbed, and Lucy faints into George Emerson's arms, thinking "Oh, what have I done?" (*R*, p. 49) as she is initiated into sexuality: "Even as she caught sight of him he grew dim; the palace itself grew dim, swayed above her, fell on to her softly, slowly, noiselessly, and the sky fell with it" (*R*, p. 49). The dying man trying to say "Live!" communicates his message to both Lucy and George [9] and begins to open the doors of their prisons.[10]

Both of them are aware of having crossed some boundary:

> She had been in his arms, and he remembered it, just as he remembered the blood on the photographs that she had bought in Alinari's shop. It was not exactly that a man had died; something

---

8. McDowell, *Forster*, p. 54.   9. Howarth, Nov. 8, 1967.
10. Trilling, *Forster*, p. 100, sees George imprisoned by his "deep, neurotic *fin de siècle* pessimism" and Lucy by her "respectability"; after the murder George wants to live and "Lucy's dull propriety begins to give way to the possibility of passion."

had happened to the living: they had come to a situation where character tells, and where Childhood enters upon the branching paths of Youth.

[R, p. 53]

The photographs with which Lucy has tried to buy liberty are covered with the blood of the dying Italian, blood which gives the knowledge of sexuality to both Lucy and George and the will to live to George: nudity plus blood equals life. George crosses his boundary when he throws away the bloody photographs and tells Lucy he has done so: "the boy verged into a man" (R, p. 51). Lucy realizes at this point that it is "hopeless to look for chivalry in such a man" (R, p. 52); she does not yet know that this is a positive evaluation.

We are impressed not that he throws away the pictures but that he tells her why he has done it, treating her as a person, a human being, rather than the "Eternal Woman" who must be protected from a knowledge of life. They emerge from prison together, and their new freedom implies equality between the sexes as well as sexuality:

It was useless to say to him, "And would you—" and hope that he would complete the sentence for himself, averting his eyes from her nakedness like the knight in that beautiful picture.

[R, pp. 52–53]

Here, George does not avert his eyes from the nakedness of Lucy's soul; later, Lucy does not avert her eyes from the nakedness of George's body. They are not knight and lady; they are man and woman.

Lucy does not find it easy to accept a womanhood which includes liberty and emancipation. For the first time she must replace propriety and societal judgment with personal judgment: she must make moral choices for herself, decide for herself what is right and wrong (R, pp. 54–55). The new Lucy judges people differently: Miss Lavish and the Reverend Mr. Eager "were tried by some new test, and they were found wanting" (*R*, p. 62). Lucy's rebellion expresses itself in words for the first time in her life when she courageously defends Mr. Emerson by challenging Mr. Eager's slander (*R*, p. 63). However, her change is not complete, and she retreats back into prison. She loses her courage, backs down (*R*, p. 64), becomes frightened of sex, and feels guilty about even the verbal intimacy established with George by the river (*R*, p. 70). Lucy tries to escape George and her new life, represented by Florence; she tries to go to Rome, where Cecil Vyse and his mother, whom she knows from home, are staying. Ironically, Charlotte does not let her go because all the arrangements have been made for a drive in the hills; Charlotte, even this early, is working toward Lucy's ultimate acceptance of George, for on this expedition he kisses her.

After the kiss, Lucy wants to talk to George, person to person, but Charlotte is horrified and can think only in terms of insulted damsel and dragon (*R*, p. 88). Yet Lucy is allowed to sublimate her heterosexual feelings for George in a homosexual embrace with Charlotte (*R*, p. 90); Charlotte, not George, takes advantage of her: "Lucy was suffering from the most grievous wrong which this world has yet discovered: diplomatic advantage had been taken of her sincerity, of her craving for sympathy and love" (*R*, p. 93). Clearly, the forces of manipulation and repression are more dangerous than the forces of sexuality, which society so fears. We are dismayed when Lucy becomes engaged to Cecil Vyse, a medieval character (*R*, p. 99).

Lucy's engagement to Cecil causes her to distort the past and her real feelings for George (*R*, p. 189), for her "engagement" is a Herbert Pembroke engagement rather than a Stewart Ansell one: cold, impersonal, institutionalized, it has nothing to do with desire. Lucy's brother Freddy seems to realize this, for he calls Cecil Lucy's "fiasco" rather than "fiancé" (*R*, p. 109). Freddy's feeling that Cecil would never wear another fellow's cap (*R*, p. 98) is an even more damning evaluation, for Cecil has no sense of "fratribus." He is a snob who condescends to Surrey society and does not understand Lucy's tolerance of it; he does not realize "that if she was too great for this society, she was too great for all society, and had reached the stage where personal intercourse would alone satisfy her" (*R*, p. 128). Lucy needs intercourse between two "persons," not between a knight and a medieval lady, and thus her relationship with Cecil is doomed.

Our introduction to Cecil is indirect. He asks Lucy's mother and brother for permission to marry Lucy (*R*, pp. 95–96), an archaic act which surprises them as much as it surprises us and which vastly amuses Mrs. Honeychurch, for Cecil prides himself on being "unconventional." Freddy's answer is straightforward: "Take her or leave her; it's no business of mine!"; and Mrs. Honeychurch's answer, "though more normal in its wording, had been to the same effect" (*R*, p. 96). Unlike Cecil, they both realize it's Lucy's decision, and they immediately establish themselves as sympathetic characters.

Cecil as a medieval character is essentially ascetic (*R*, p. 100), and the "depths of prudishness within him" (*R*, p. 123) give him a conventional view of love: "he believed that women revere men for their manliness" (*R*, p. 124). He tries to "protect" Lucy from George's nakedness because of a misguided, chivalric belief "that he must lead women, though he knew not whither, and protect them, though he knew not against what" (*R*, p. 152). Cecil accepts the double standard, and Lucy doesn't dare tell him about George's kiss: "she knew in her heart that she could not trust him, for he desired her untouched" (*R*, p. 169)—although it is perfectly all right for him to have had a girlfriend (*R*, p. 139).

Cecil's medievalism manifests itself in antifeminism as well as asceticism. He patronizes women and laughs at Lucy's "feminine inconsequence" (*R*, p. 113). Believing "that a woman's power and charm reside in mystery, not in muscular rant" (*R,* p. 114), he pays no attention to anything she says: "Charm, not argument, was to be her forte" (*R,* p. 179). To Cecil, Lucy is a possession, and she is compared to two villas "acquired by Sir Harry Otway the very afternoon that Lucy had been acquired by Cecil" (*R,* p. 116). When Lucy tries to establish the Miss Alans in those villas, Cecil thwarts her plans; he doesn't mind inconveniencing women or making Lucy look ridiculous (*R,* p. 135). His attitude is that of medieval overlord: "the only relationship which Cecil conceived was feudal: that of protector and protected. He had no glimpse of the comradeship after which the girl's soul yearned" (*R,* p. 179), a comradeship which George does offer.

Unlike George, Cecil has no intention of viewing Lucy as a whole person, or even a person at all. He sees her rather as a work of art (*R,* p. 110) and tries to fit her into an impossible, inhuman mold. His aestheticism seems in large part due to his London upbringing, and Lucy is impressed by the "witty weariness" of the talk at a London dinner party (*R,* p. 140). She realizes, however, that her married life in London "would estrange her a little from all that she had loved in the past" (*R,* p. 140). While Cecil connects Lucy with "a view," she connects him with a room, a drawing-room "with no view" (*R,* p. 122). Life in London is a nightmare, as Lucy's subconscious realizes when she cries out in her sleep in the Vyse's London flat; she awakens "with her hand on her cheek" (*R,* p. 141), reminding us of George's kiss and contrasting her anticipated life with Cecil to a freer, more natural one with George.

When Lucy sees George for the first time in England, she immediately knows that he has not told his father about their kiss, that he does not consider her an "exploit" (*R,* p. 178). George's awkwardness in front of Charlotte endears him to Lucy:

men were not gods after all, but as human and as clumsy as girls; even men might suffer from unexplained desires, and need help.

To one of her upbringing, and of her destination, the weakness of
men was a truth unfamiliar, but she had surmised it at Florence,
when George threw her photographs into the river Arno.

[R, p. 178]

Because of George, Lucy can for the moment react individ-
ually and personally, not according to the sex stereotypes
Cecil demands. But Lucy can not yet accept her love for
George and attempts to stifle it, with the aid of Charlotte
(R, p. 188), the novel's prime example of the unloved and
the unlovable.

Like Rickie Elliot in *The Longest Journey,* Lucy lives in an
unreal world: "The contest lay not between love and duty.
Perhaps there never is such a contest. It lay between the
real and the pretended, and Lucy's first aim was to defeat
herself" (R, p. 188). Her brain clouds over (R, p. 188), reminding us of Rickie's "cloud of unreality" (LJ, p. 191)
when he is with Agnes. Lucy takes on Charlotte's values and
Agnes's brutality when she reacts to George's second kiss as
to an insult, declares him a cad, and asserts, "What's wanted
is a man with a whip" (R, p. 191). It is ironic that she considers *George* brutal at the very moment she herself exhibits
the real brutality of propriety. Fortunately, her anger fades
at the sight of him, a sight which produces a rush in her
blood (R, p. 192). Physical sight is important in *A Room with
a View,* and here it reminds us of Lucy's view of George
naked. Lucy should have seen George after their first kiss in
Florence also, for much muddle could have been avoided.

Lucy is not yet clear of muddle, however; Charlotte's influence is still strong and still seems on the side of repression. Although George is the ideal emancipated lover and
tells Lucy, "I want you to have your own thoughts even
when I hold you in my arms" (R, p. 195), she tells him she
loves Cecil. We do not believe her, since the chapter is titled
"Lying to George" (R, p. 188). When Lucy rejects George,
the novel's tone becomes dark. Lucy herself suddenly be-

comes aware of autumn, and this awareness echoes verbally what is said earlier about Miss Alan.[11]

George's analysis of Cecil is quite astute:

[Cecil] daren't let a woman decide. He's the type who's kept Europe back for a thousand years. Every moment of his life he's forming you, telling you what's charming or amusing or ladylike, telling you what a man thinks womanly; and you, you of all women, listen to his voice instead of your own.

[*R*, p. 194]

He does not condemn Cecil, because he understands him. He says, "I'm the same kind of brute at bottom. This desire to govern a woman—it lies very deep, and men and women must fight it together before they shall enter the garden" (*R*, p. 195). Although Lucy cannot yet admit that she loves George, she does immediately break her engagement with Cecil, and in her rejection incorporates much of what George has said:

I won't be protected. I will choose for myself what is ladylike and right. To shield me is an insult. Can't I be trusted to face the truth but I must get it second-hand through you? A woman's place!

[*R*, p. 201]

The real insult is to be protected, not to be kissed; but at this point Lucy realizes only the first of these two facts. Eventually she becomes able to accept both freedom and sexuality, and realize that only Cecil, not George, has insulted her.

Lucy denies breaking off her engagement because of another man and furiously gives Cecil the feminist argument that everyone thinks "women are always thinking of men": "As if a girl can't break it off for the sake of freedom" (*R*, pp. 202–3). A slight problem arises here, however, for

11. Trilling, *Forster*, pp. 107–8.

Lucy really is breaking it off for the sake of another man, although she will not yet admit it. Either Lucy is simply deluding herself, or George is functioning in the novel as "freedom"—not just another man, but another style of life.

Cecil takes his rejection well and admits that Lucy is right in her analysis of him: "I have never known you till this evening. I have just used you as a peg for my silly notions of what a woman should be" (*R*, p. 202). Unfortunately, that is the paradigm for most male-female relations, as we see in *The Longest Journey* in Rickie and Agnes's relationship. Most people, like Cecil, react only to role stereotypes, not to individuals, and thus George and the Emerson "view" of personal relations seems even more attractive by comparison.

Lucy is not yet ready to reject role stereotypes entirely, however. Although she does reject Cecil's, Lucy impales herself on feminist rhetoric and a feminist stereotype: "She could never marry. . . . She must be one of the women whom she had praised so eloquently, who care for liberty and not for men; she must forget that George loved her" (*R*, p. 204). Her decision not to marry is stupid, for she overlooks the most important thing the Emersons stand for, the Yes of personal relations. Lucy must learn not to act according to theory, or principle, or convention—Charlotte's way—but according to individual people and specific events—the Emerson way; and she must learn this before she can accept George. To Forster, connected personal intercourse is what counts. Lucy and George's love is more important than feminist theory, just as it is more important than Cecil's medieval theory. Feminist theory is not invalidated thereby any more than Lucy's criticism of Cecil and of his view of women is invalidated by her love for George.

Lucy temporarily joins "the vast armies of the benighted, who follow neither the heart nor the brain, and march to their destiny by catch-words" (*R*, p. 204). Forster attributes her flirtation with the abyss to pretense, to a lack of reality that again recalls *The Longest Journey:*

Lucy entered this army when she pretended to George that she
did not love him, and pretended to Cecil that she loved no one.
The night received her, as it had received Miss Bartlett thirty
years before.

[*R*, p. 204]

Lucy's voice becomes hard, and she starts to resemble a
mixture of the worst elements of Charlotte Bartlett and
Eleanor Lavish: she is irritable, petulant, and anxious to do
the unexpected (*R*, p. 226). She dangles over the brink of
Miss Alandom when she almost goes to Greece with those
two women to escape George a second time, but she is saved
by "the true chivalry—not the worn-out chivalry of sex, but
the true chivalry that all the young may show to all the old"
(*R*, p. 235): she cannot lie to Mr. Emerson. Her false feminist rhetoric falls away at his statement of specific fact, a
statement which reveals his intuitive grasp of the situation:

"Oh, how like a man!—I mean, to suppose that a woman is always
thinking about a man."
    "But you are."

[*R*, p. 237]

When he forces her to view specifics, all the muddle disappears, and a truer feminism emerges, truer because it is
humanism. Sexual equality, like everything else, must be
approached through personal relations, and Mr. Emerson
gives Lucy the "feeling that, in gaining the man she loved,
she would gain something for the whole world" (*R*, p. 240).

At the end of the novel, Lucy achieves happiness and
equality with George, but at the price of a break with her
family:

His own content was absolute, but hers held bitterness: the Honeychurches had not forgiven them; they were disgusted at her
past hypocrisy; she had alienated Windy Corner, perhaps for
ever.

[*R*, p. 243]

This alienation is upsetting, for Windy Corner is the happiest home Forster ever shows us, and the Honeychurches have an excellent family relationship. The rift is particularly sad because we are told that Mrs. Honeychurch and Freddy get along very well with George, much better than they do with Cecil. Charlotte, who is ultimately responsible for bringing Lucy and George together, is indirectly responsible for alienating Lucy from her family. What the Honeychurches cannot forgive is hypocrisy, and "Left to herself, Lucy would have told her mother and her lover ingenuously [about George's kiss], and it would have remained a little thing" (*R,* p. 139).

Although Mrs. Honeychurch represents the good side of Mrs. Herriton of *Where Angels Fear to Tread,* amenable, amusing, and kind, we must hold her rather than Charlotte finally responsible for the break with Lucy. Mrs. Honeychurch exhibits several serious character flaws: she does not trust passion (*R,* p. 37), and she is vehemently antifeminist, both traits which link her to Cecil. Mrs. Honeychurch, despised by Cecil as conventional and mundane, is just as concerned over "woman's place" as he is, a fact which may in itself require a break from an emancipated Lucy. Mrs. Honeychurch essentially does not like women (*R,* p. 120), and she sets very narrow limits on their acceptable roles. She judges other women primarily as domestics and criticizes Cecil's mother for being a bad housekeeper (*R,* p. 98). Mrs. Honeychurch does not believe that women should work outside the home at all, and they especially should not write; she is both antifeminist and antiliterary:

nothing roused Mrs. Honeychurch so much as literature in the hands of females. She would abandon every topic to inveigh against those women who (instead of minding their houses and their children) seek notoriety by print. Her attitude was: "If books must be written, let them be written by men."

[*R,* p. 160]

Although Mrs. Honeychurch wants to limit other women to a purely domestic life, she herself is in an unusually free position. Like Mrs. Herriton, she is the head of her house and has no husband to tell her what to do, to constrict her to what she sees as "woman's place." Yet, like Mrs. Herriton, she has totally internalized society's conventional roles and would probably not be able to accept a free and equal alliance for her daughter even if Charlotte had not intervened. Her first reaction to even hearing the Emerson name is negative: "I trusted they were no relations of Emerson the philosopher, a most trying man" (*R,* p. 131). She is the only character to make this connection, a connection Forster wants us to make in a more positive manner.

Mr. Emerson's view that "Marriage is a duty" (*R,* p. 146) is the view of the novel as a whole, and in this *A Room with a View* is unique among Forster's novels. It successfully overcomes those personal "limitations" which Rickie Elliot asserts (*LJ,* p. 296) need not intrude in literature, for *A Room with a View* is an effective paean to heterosexual love and marriage. The marriage of which Mr. Emerson speaks, however, is not the conventional, oppressive institution, but rather the ultimate personal relation between two equal individuals, a relation which includes "tenderness," "comradeship," and "poetry" (*R,* p. 237). Although this sort of relationship is not always intrinsically heterosexual, as we see in *Maurice,* it is so in *A Room with a View;* the only (ambiguously) homosexual character, Mr. Beebe,[12] represents the forces of darkness and Pauline antisexuality (*R,* pp. 218–19), which fight the Emersonian forces of light and passion.

The Emerson view prevails, and at the end of *A Room with*

12. Crews, *Perils of Humanism,* p. 85*n*7, wonders if "Mr. Beebe's position is homosexual as well as doctrinal?" and then quotes *A Room with a View,* p. 38: "Girls like Lucy were charming to look at, but Mr. Beebe was, from rather profound reasons, somewhat chilly in his attitude towards the other sex, and preferred to be interested rather than enthralled."

a View Lucy and George are married and happy. They return to the Pension Bertolini from their honeymoon to
begin their married life in Mr. Emerson's old room, for
they have both accepted his view of life and can now accept
his Yes; the final chapter is titled "The End of the Middle
Ages." They play like children, and when Lucy calls George
a baby (*R*, p. 242), we fear that they're going to enact the
mother-child roles we saw between Caroline Abbott and
both Philip and Gino in *Where Angels Fear to Tread*. The love
between Lucy and George does not deteriorate into that,
however, for they have both grown beyond arbitrary roles.
Lucy states this explicitly when she finds fault with Cecil for
becoming cynical about women: "Why will men have
theories about women? I haven't any about men"
(*R*, p. 243); personal relations finally triumph for Lucy and
George.

   One last obstacle must be overcome before their triumph
is complete, however. Lucy does not accede to total liberation easily; she is a heroine, not a hero. Almost our final
view of Lucy shows her mending George's sock (*R*, p. 242),
and indeed Frederick Crews sees this as *the* final view when
he says, "It is worth remembering that Lucy, who finally
embodies Forster's idea of the happy modern woman, is last
seen in the act of mending her husband's socks"; [13] but
what follows is crucially important. George, in a symbolic
rejection of the old arbitrary roles, tells Lucy to forget about
the sock, and he carries her over to the window "so that she,
too, saw all the view" (*R*, p. 244). The final image of the
book is of a view and a song, for "they heard the river, bear-
ing down the snows of winter into the Mediterranean"
(*R*, p. 246); the melting snows give us hope for the future.

13. Crews, *Perils of Humanism*, p. 87.

Four
Howards End

This novel is "Forster's masterpiece." [1] Its epigraph and theme, "Only connect . . . ," is the theme of all Forster's novels; and the route to connection in *Howards End,* as in all the novels, is personal intercourse, a term which may be understood both sexually and socially. Sexually, connection must take place in two ways: within individuals and between individuals. Each person must accept sexuality internally by connecting his or her own "beast" side with his or her own "monk" side (*HE,* p. 187) before connecting externally with others. Socially, connection must take place in an atmosphere of equality between the sexes, and *Howards End* attempts to resolve that problem also. The heroes in this novel are two particular women who are superior to the particular men they encounter, although, in the society at large, women are by definition inferior. Forster's heroes go beyond the superiority or inferiority of one sex or one class; they strive to reach the *personal,* where each person is only an individual and can therefore connect with any other individual.

The most important point of *Howards End,* and of all Forster's novels, is that people are individually different. One must not allow oneself to be defined by expected role stereotypes, for individual differences matter more than role differences, class differences, or sex differences; and personal intercourse, in both its senses, must be allowed to reflect this individuality. Margaret and Helen Schlegel, the

1. Trilling, *Forster,* p. 114.

two heroes of *Howards End,* exemplify two unique personalities and two kinds of personal intercourse and connection. Margaret's marriage to Henry Wilcox, uniting the intellectual middle class with the dynamic industrial upper middle class, is both physical and emotional; while Helen's union with Leonard Bast, the novel's borderline-lower-class character, unites the lower and middle classes but is purely physical. When Helen feels guilty for her inability to love a man, as Margaret loves Henry, Margaret states that she herself does not love children and feels no need to. She articulates Forster's greatest theme:

It is only that people are far more different than is pretended. All over the world men and women are worrying because they cannot develop as they are supposed to develop. . . . Develop what you have. . . . Differences—eternal differences, planted by God in a single family, so that there may always be colour; sorrow perhaps, but colour in the daily grey.

[*HE,* pp. 337–38]

Eternal differences are individual, not arbitary.

Margaret Schlegel, the primary hero, achieves an internal connection which accepts sexuality and then transcends sexual differences.[2] Attempting to help her husband connect the two sides of *his* nature and overcome his belief "that bodily passion is bad" (*HE,* p. 186), she proves her heroism when she tries to build "the rainbow bridge that should connect the prose in us with the passion" (*HE,* p. 186). Margaret connects prose and passion, masculine and feminine; her "androgynous mind"[3] transcends sex, as do the symbolic wych-elm and the house itself.[4]

2. Trilling, ibid, p. 135, considers Margaret and Helen inadequate because they do not conform to their roles, and, p. 126, sees *Howards End* as a story of a sex war, "the war between men and women"; but Crews's analysis, *Perils of Humanism,* p. 113, is more convincing: "*Howards End* is a novel about reconciling the feminine with the masculine nature."

3. Edgerton, "The Androgynous Mind," p. 68.

4. J. B. Beer, *The Achievement of E. M. Forster* (New York, Barnes and Noble, 1962), p. 126.

Margaret is Forster's quintessential androgynous hero and connects the themes of all of his novels: the acceptance of sexuality, the role of women (and by extension of homosexuals) in society, and the importance of fraternity. Margaret's version of "fratribus" may be called "sororibus" for want of a better name (and to continue Forster's dative), but it is not only for women, as the brotherhood of *Where Angels Fear to Tread* and *The Longest Journey* is only for men. Sororibus is bisexual and androgynous; and it is connected and reconciled to (hetero)sexual love and marriage at the end of *Howards End.*

Marriage itself, however, presents Margaret with certain problems. In *The Longest Journey,* Rickie's marriage robs him of his independence; in *Howards End,* Margaret faces a similar threat. Forster's statement that "She was to keep her independence more than do most women as yet" (*HE,* p. 174) implies that she does not keep it totally, and also that women tend to lose more by marriage than men do. Although Forster recognizes the oppression of women as the more institutionalized, he insists that the danger exists regardless of sex and is part of the institution of marriage: both partners must guard against oppression and "the astonishing glass shade" which "interposes between married couples and the world" (*HE,* p. 174). Helen astutely asserts that if anyone can "pull it off," can make the institution of marriage work, Margaret can, for Margaret is heroic (*HE,* p. 194). The Schlegel sisters are not strident reformers, and their belief in sexual equality (*HE,* p. 28) is acted on in their personal relations with men, with the emphasis always on the personal:

She must remain herself, for his sake as well as her own, since a shadowy wife degrades the husband whom she accompanies, and she must assimilate for reasons of common honesty, since she had no right to marry a man and make him uncomfortable.

[*HE,* pp. 221–22]

Margaret's goal is clear, and she achieves it in the reconciliation at the end of the novel.[5]

The critical reaction to the ending of *Howards End* is
strongly antifeminist.[6] Henry is not "gelded" or "humiliated," however; he is rather more human than ever before.
Throughout the novel, he never worries about women
being oppressed, but at the end he is concerned over an
equal relationship: he finally connects. Helen is reconciled
with Henry, for they both "learnt to understand one another and to forgive" (*HE*, p. 338), and it is Margaret who
settles them down. Comradeship and sororibus are reconciled, for sisterhood is shown to be necessary to make the
comradeship of marriage work. At the end, Margaret connects the prose and the passion externally, Henry as the
prose and Helen as the passion. The final scene convinces:
the prose and the passion are truly both "exalted," and
"human love" is "seen at its height" (*HE*, p. 187). The final
vision is androgynous, and it is crucially important that no
one, and no one sex, "controls" anything.[7]

Howards End explores the attempt of Margaret and Helen
Schlegel "to see life steadily and to see it whole." The
Schlegel search for the good moral life was begun by their
father, who is probably the single most important influence
on Margaret's life. "Schlegel" is a masculine noun in German which means mallet, club, or drum-stick, and the beating of a drum is a recurring image in the novel. Margaret
and Helen's brother Tibby, who is only minimally influ-

5. The problem of marriage in *The Longest Journey* is further resolved in *Howards
End*, where, as Beer maintains, *Achievement*, p. 129, "the androgynous union of
qualities within the heroine which overarches and includes all other unions" provides "greater stability and wider relevance" than a "simple romantic marriage."
6. Trilling, *Forster*, p. 135, for example, finds the ending unsatisfactory because
"the male is too thoroughly gelded," and Frank Tuohy, "The English Question,"
Spectator, 219 (July 6, 1962), 30–31, feels "something voracious in Margaret as she
sits beside her humiliated Henry." Tuohy also sees Mrs. Wilcox as "unconsciously
sadistic as she keeps carrying that wisp of hay towards her hay-fever prone family."
7. Trilling, *Forster*, p. 134, mistakenly asserts that at the end of the book the "Eternal Feminine" is taking "complete control of England."

enced by their father, nevertheless notes "the transitional passage on the drum" (*HE,* p. 33) in Beethoven's Fifth Symphony. Later in the novel, Miss Avery, the heart of Howards End, is introduced by a beating sound, by "A noise as of drums" (*HE,* p. 202), and she also is connected with transitions.[8]

The Schlegel upbringing is unique. Their mother is barely mentioned; we know only that she had money (*HE,* p. 29), and that she died in childbirth when Tibby was born and Margaret was "but thirteen" (*HE,* p. 13). Margaret takes over the role of mother at that time: she refuses Aunt Juley's offer of surrogate motherhood then and again five years later, when their father dies. When the novel opens, Margaret is playing mother to Tibby and is prevented from visiting the Wilcoxes by his illness (*HE,* p. 7). Indeed, she is both father and mother to him, for she combines the influence of both Germany and England, the fatherland and the mother country.

The Schlegel girls receive a unique and very liberal education, one which imparts to Margaret an abiding trust in individuals (*HE,* p. 30). "Helen advanced along the same lines, though with a more irresponsible tread. In character she resembled her sister, but she was pretty, and so apt to have a more amusing time" (*HE,* p. 30–31). As with Lilia in *Where Angels Fear to Tread,* good looks in *Howards End* are largely detrimental: they are too easy to fall back on, for

looks have their influence upon character. The sisters were alike as little girls, but at the time of the Wilcox episode their methods were beginning to diverge; the younger was rather apt to entice people, and, in enticing them, to be herself enticed; the elder went straight ahead, and accepted an occasional failure as part of the game.

[*HE,* p. 31]

8. Thomson, *Fiction,* p. 186, points out that "Miss Avery, descending the stairs, marks the transition in the house—from Ruth Wilcox to Margaret Schlegel." He further notes that "the heart of the house beats 'faintly at first,' suggesting Mrs. Wilcox, 'then loudly, martially,' suggesting Margaret."

Tibby, unlike his sisters, does not inherit the best of his father; like Cecil Vyse in *A Room with a View,* he represents culture without feeling: [9] "He was frigid, through no fault of his own, and without cruelty" (*HE,* p. 280). When Tibby asserts that he does not want a profession, Margaret refers specifically to a "Mr. Vyse" (*HE,* p. 109) as an example of a man who does not work and is not happy, and to a "Mr. Pembroke" (*HE,* p. 111) as an example of a man who does work and is the better for it. Margaret's belief in work is related to her attraction to Mr. Wilcox, but it also expresses the heart of feminism:

I believe that in the last century men have developed the desire for work, and they must not starve it. It's a new desire. It goes with a great deal that's bad, but in itself it's good, and I hope that for women too, "not to work" will soon become as shocking as "not to be married" was a hundred years ago.

[*HE,* p. 110]

Margaret does not want to be a parasite of sex or of class, and her definition of heaven includes "activity without civilization," which sounds Shavian, as does Tibby's of hell: "civilization without activity" (*HE,* p. 112). Tibby's desire for civilization is fulfilled at Oxford, but at an aesthete's Oxford, without fraternity (*HE,* p. 106). Oxford cannot give Tibby what Cambridge gives other male Forster characters, but at least it is open to him; only minimal opportunity for a university education exists for Margaret and Helen, who clearly would be better able to use it.

Class and money play important roles in *Howards End,* and the Schlegels believe in equality between the classes as much as in equality between the sexes. Like Mr. Emerson in *A Room with a View,* however, they do not blind themselves to the differences caused by different upbringings, and they are radical in their recognition of the power of money:

9. Howarth, Nov. 8, 1967.

these were women with a theory, who held that reticence about money matters is absurd, and that life would be truer if each would state the exact size of the golden island upon which he stands, the exact stretch of warp over which he throws the woof that is not money. How can we do justice to the pattern otherwise?

[*HE*, p. 141]

Margaret sees a direct link between money and liberalism: "independent thoughts are in nine cases out of ten the result of independent means" (*HE*, p. 127). In the theoretical discussion group which attempts to dispose of a hypothetical millionaire's legacy, Margaret ignores idealism and "political economy" in favor of the personal: "she only fixed her eyes on a few human beings, to see how, under present conditions, they could be made happier" (*HE*, p. 128). Her answer is to give cash: "Money: give Mr. Bast money, and don't bother about his ideals. He'll pick up those for himself" (*HE*, p. 127).

The particular Mr. Bast under discussion is not hypothetical. Leonard Bast is the living representative of the nearness of the abyss of poverty in *Howards End* (*HE*, p. 45), and Forster's portrayal of him is brilliant. The image of Leonard trying to talk culture while thinking of his "stolen" umbrella is unforgettable, and it connects him with Schlegel père, for "Behind Monet and Debussy the umbrella persisted, with the steady beat of a drum" (*HE*, p. 40). Leonard is killed by Mr. Schlegel's sword immediately after accepting the tapping of the drums that accompany the goblins Helen hears in Beethoven (*HE*, p. 324).

Leonard achieves nobility by walking all night and discovering for himself that the dawn is not wonderful (*HE*, p. 119); and afterward, "That the Schlegels had not thought him foolish became a permanent joy" (*HE*, p. 124). This links him to Conrad's Lord Jim, another failed hero who gets his idea of romance and heroism from literature, since Forster's quotation from "the mystic," "My conviction

. . . gains infinitely the moment another soul will believe in it" (*HE,* p. 124), is the Novalis epigraph to *Lord Jim.* Because the Schlegels believe in Leonard's walk, "the heart of a man" ticked in his chest (*HE,* p. 125); because Marlow believes in Jim, Jim attains manhood among the Malays. Like Jim, Leonard cannot connect romance with life, and he dooms himself when he says, "I fail to see the connection" (*HE,* p. 143).

Leonard's marriage to Jacky is pathetic, characterized by "Petulance and squalor" (*HE,* p. 123), and he stays with her only out of chivalry (*HE,* p. 54). Although he is not antifeminist and cooks dinner for himself and Jacky (*HE,* p. 53), Leonard nevertheless accepts and is the victim of the sexual myth of male dominance that is concomitant with chivalry. He blames himself for "seducing" Helen (*HE,* p. 316), and it never occurs to him that Helen may have instigated proceedings. When he dies, he has not been told that he is about to be a father, and his last words are to Margaret: "Mrs. Wilcox . . . I have done wrong" (*HE,* p. 324). The cause of death is heart disease (*HE,* p. 326), but Leonard's is not the only diseased heart, and Miss Avery declares his death to be murder (*HE,* p. 325). A society which would consider poor pathetic Leonard a seducer surely does have a disease of the heart, and Charles Wilcox's heart in particular is undeveloped. His brutal reaction to Leonard, whom he has never even seen, is to want to "thrash him within an inch of his life" (*HE,* p. 324). Charles, and to a lesser extent Henry Wilcox, exhibit the most acute "heart disease" in the novel.

Leonard's wife Jacky combines the themes of class and sex: she is oppressed by both, for she belongs to the class society calls "lower" and the sex it considers inferior. She functions essentially as a connection: Henry Wilcox is to Jacky as Helen is to Leonard. As a lower-class woman used by an upper-middle-class man, Jacky has few options open to her, and her only out is to latch on to a lower-middle-class man, resulting in a sad situation for all concerned. Jacky's belief that marriage will make everything all right (*HE*, p. 53) stresses the fact that for the poor, marriage is an economic, not a spiritual, state. A problem for the Schlegels, marriage is considered the ultimate good by poor Jacky. Women like Jacky are the price society pays for its double standard and its double view of women; she is used, discarded, and condemned, a clearly unfair treatment for any human being. Helen blames men for Jacky's plight rather than blaming her (*HE*, p. 237), a radical view that Forster accepts.

The Schlegels' Aunt Juley Munt, an upper-middle-class matron, receives all the benefits society gives rich women and thus poses an interesting contrast to Jacky Bast. Mrs. Munt's life reflects the uselessness of Mrs. Herriton's, and her offer to act as Margaret's messenger in the Helen and Paul affair reveals much about her:

"Dear, I have nothing to call me back to Swanage." She spread out her plump arms. "I am all at your disposal. Let me go down to this house whose name I forget instead of you."

[*HE*, p. 9]

Margaret's belief in work is relevant here, for Aunt Juley's having no reason to go home implies that England provides no satisfactory role for an older, widowed, or otherwise single woman with no children, or whose children are grown, except to meddle in the affairs of the young. Her plump arms are clearly necessary for her to be an effective aunt, but her forgetting the name of Howards End is a very bad sign. She calls it different things at different times, "Howards House" (*HE*, p. 11) at one point and "Howards Lodge" (*HE*, p. 15) at another. We should not condemn her too much, however. Her inability to grasp the end of the Howards may imply that their yeoman life is still alive to her, since she does live in the country.

Aunt Juley's opinions of the Schlegels give us a helpful contrast between typical British and the atypical Schlegels. Aunt Juley is narrow, conservative, and nationalistic; not surprisingly, she finds her nieces too liberal and democratic (*HE*, p. 14), and unfortunately German. The Schlegels' German cousin Frieda Mosebach is Aunt Juley's counterpart. Her very name suggests "mossback," and she is indeed conservative and extremely chauvinistic.

The offhand opening line of *Howards End* informs us of the importance of Helen Schlegel's point of view: "One may as well begin with Helen's letters to her sister" (*HE*, p. 3); and the novel ends with Helen's child and Helen's view of the future: "We've seen to the very end, and it'll be such a crop of hay as never!" (*HE*, p. 343). She is the first Schlegel to fall under the charm of the Wilcox men; as she does so, she loses her judgment and is convinced by specious arguments of the truth of ideas we know to be false:

I couldn't point to a time when men had been equal, nor even to a time when the wish to be equal had made them happier in other ways. I couldn't say a word. I had just picked up the notion that equality is good from some book—probably from poetry, or you. Anyhow, it's been knocked into pieces.

[*HE*, pp. 5–6]

When she writes to Margaret that she has fallen in love with Paul (*HE*, p. 6), we are suspicious, for she has already shown a lack of judgment. Helen tends to depersonalize people, to see them as representative or ideal, and she sees Paul as Romance (*HE*, p. 24), as Leonard Bast is later to see her. Helen's "abandonment of personality that is a possible prelude to love" (*HE*, p. 24) anticipates the effect of the caves in *A Passage to India*.

Helen's approach to sex is active rather than passive, and she meets Paul more than halfway (*HE*, p. 24), but her sexual liberation is here tied up with its social converse, her enjoyment of domination by the Wilcoxes. The sexual act itself has meaning for Helen, apart from the man connected with it, as we see here with Paul and later with Leonard:

To Helen, at all events, her life was to bring nothing more intense than the embrace of this boy who played no part in it. . . . A man in the darkness, he had whispered: "I love you" when she was desiring love. In time his slender personality faded, the scene that he had evoked endured. In all the variable years that followed she never saw the like of it again.

[*HE*, p. 25]

When Helen has sexual intercourse with Leonard Bast, he is "not a man, but a cause" (*HE*, p. 311), for "Helen loved the absolute. Leonard had been ruined absolutely, . . . and she loved him absolutely, perhaps for half an hour" (*HE*, pp. 316–17). The physical manifestation of her acceptance of Mr. Emerson's transitory Yes is equally transitory, but this does not make it less affirmative. The critical reaction to the sexual intercourse between Helen and Leonard is rather peculiar; for some reason, most critics speak of Helen as passively "giving herself" [10] to Leonard, as if she were a chocolate bar or a cup of tea. Apparently, it is as inconceivable to most critics as it is to Leonard that a woman should make sexual advances to a man, especially to a man with whom she has no intention of establishing a permanent relationship. Yet no one except Margaret has any trouble believing that Henry has made sexual advances to Jacky, and Helen is a much more connected and passionate person than Henry.

Henry's "manliness," which enables critics to accept *his* affair, is a trait that has only negative effects when reflected in Paul (*HE*, p. 26). The whole Wilcox idea of masculinity rests upon lack of fear, for fear is considered feminine; but fear and bravery are human emotions, not sexual ones. Men like Mr. Schlegel and George Emerson in *A Room with a View*, who are human and male rather than chivalrous and

10. For example, Trilling, *Forster*, p. 132, and McDowell, *Forster*, p. 95.

"manly," are quite able to feel frightened without falling apart. After her experience at the Wilcoxes', Helen trusts in personal relations and the inner life (*HE,* p. 28), for she has learned a valuable lesson: the reality of a panic and emptiness which hitherto have been merely hypothetical.

Helen first speaks of "panic and emptiness" (*HE,* p. 26) after her disillusionment with Paul, and panic here is the negative side of nature, the opposite of the positive hay. Panic derives from the destructive Pan of *The Longest Journey* and is reflected in "culture" also in *Howards End.* The most memorable image in the novel is that of the goblins in Beethoven's Fifth Symphony who "merely observed in passing that there was no such thing as splendour or heroism in the world" (*HE,* p. 33). *Howards End* gains much of its force from the fact that everything takes place in a very modern world where the goblins may return at any time. Forster's goblins parallel Conrad's heart of darkness: Marlow's heroism consists of being able to enter the heart of darkness, know it, yet emerge and continue to exist with that knowledge; and Margaret is a kind of Marlow.

Margaret recognizes the Wilcox flaws, but she also recognizes their virtues:

They led a life that she could not attain to—the outer life of "telegrams and anger." . . . To Margaret this life was to remain a real force. She could not despise it, as Helen and Tibby affected to do. It fostered such virtues as neatness, decision, and obedience, virtues of the second rank, no doubt, but they have formed our civilization. They form character, too. . . . How dare Schlegels despise Wilcoxes, when it takes all sorts to make a world?

[*HE,* pp. 103–4]

Money is necessary, and the Wilcoxes do save England and Howards End,[11] as Margaret appreciates: "More and more do I refuse to draw my income and sneer at those who guarantee it" (*HE,* p. 175).

11. Carolyn Heilbrun, lecture, doctoral seminar, Columbia University, Nov. 5, 1971.

The Wilcoxes avoid the "personal note" in life (*HE,* p. 92), and Helen perceptively comments that they can't say "I" (*HE,* p. 234).[12] Charles Wilcox's marriage reflects this impersonality, and its conventionality outlines the pitfalls Margaret must avoid in her marriage to Henry: Charles calls Dolly, whose function is clear from her name, "little woman," and he grants her "All his affection and half his attention" throughout what is said to be "their happy married life" (*HE,* p. 95).

Ruth Wilcox represents the primary connection between the Schlegels and the Wilcoxes. An androgynous Demeter-figure,[13] she is immediately identified with the image of hay, which contrasts her to Charles, Henry, and Tibby, all of whom have hay fever.[14] Mrs. Wilcox is repeatedly described as wearing long trailing dresses, usually trailing on the grass or in the hay (*HE,* e.g., p. 4), contrasting her with other women who lift their skirts to avoid contact with the earth. Her most impressive characteristic is her "instinctive wisdom" of "the past" (*HE,* p. 22). Appreciating the complexity of life, Mrs. Wilcox asserts that there is no such thing as a plain question (*HE,* p. 22). Although she always sounds uncertain (*HE,* p. 69), she intuitively knows of Paul and Helen's love without being told, just as she knows when it is over.

Mrs. Wilcox's friendship with Margaret reaches its peak when she invites Margaret to Howards End after hearing that the Schlegels are about to lose their own house (*HE,* p. 83). Margaret at first refuses but soon realizes that the moment is symbolic and flies to the station just in time to catch Mrs. Wilcox (*HE,* p. 86). Their pilgrimage never takes place, however, for Mrs. Wilcox is recalled to her duties as a wife and mother by the sudden reappearance of

12. Gransden, *Forster,* p. 61, pursues this point when he states that "we have seen Wilcoxes through Schlegels' eyes (and since Wilcoxes have no eyes of their own, this is the only way they *can* be seen)."

13. McDowell, *Forster,* p. 85.

14. E. K. Brown, *Rhythm in the Novel* (Toronto, University of Toronto Press, 1950), p. 47.

her family, and the next we hear of her she has died. Charles calls her "the mater" (*HE*, p. 17) as if she does not exist outside that role, and indeed her "life had been spent in the service of husband and sons" (*HE*, p. 74). She is not a feminist at all and suggests that "it is wiser to leave action and discussion to men" (*HE*, p. 77). Out of focus with daily life (*HE*, p. 76), Mrs. Wilcox transcends feminism and sexual inequality and somehow gives "the idea of greatness" (*HE*, p. 76).

Even in death Mrs. Wilcox is connected with flowers and love, for the woodcutter steals the chrysanthemums Margaret has laid on her grave and gives them to his girlfriend (*HE*, p. 89). Ruth's connection with Margaret continues after death, for she wills Margaret Howards End (*HE*, p. 76), perhaps as a Christmas present,[15] and certainly in recognition of a spiritual heir. Mrs. Wilcox's family does her a serious disservice by not letting her die in the room where she was born, yet they view *her* action as "Treachery!" (*HE*, p. 99). Mrs. Wilcox's will like the will of Shakespeare's Caesar, triumphs in the end, however. When Margaret marries Henry, she sees Mrs. Wilcox as a "welcome ghost" (*HE*, p. 166), and Margaret herself is called "Mrs. Wilcox" in the last chapter of the novel.[16]

Margaret's reaction to Helen and Paul's love affair when the novel opens connects her with Mrs. Wilcox. Unwilling to agree with Aunt Juley that Helen and Paul's love is "too sudden" (*HE*, p. 7), Margaret exhibits an open mind when she refuses to condemn without knowledge. She repeatedly asks, "Who knows?" The answer, of course, is that Mrs. Wilcox knows and is also unwilling to condemn. Margaret understands "as much as ever is understood of these things"

15. Martial Rose, *Literature in Perspective: E. M. Forster* (London, Evans Brothers, 1970), p. 68.

16. McDowell, *Forster*, p. 85, points out that "she has now assumed Ruth Wilcox' role as mediator and peace-maker. Helen assumes Mrs. Wilcox' other role, that of mother."

(*HE*, p. 25), but we assume that Mrs. Wilcox understands even more.

Margaret feels inadequate next to Mrs. Wilcox and apologizes for what she sees as the superficiality of her luncheon for Mrs. Wilcox (*HE*, p. 78). The Schlegels' London life does indeed seem brittle in the symbolic presence of Howards End in the person of Ruth Wilcox, but Margaret is not *personally* inadequate (as is her fellow Londoner, Cecil Vyse, in *A Room with a View*). Margaret is much younger than Mrs. Wilcox and has ample room for growth; and she does remarkably well for someone without the benefits of a country upbringing. Margaret's relationship with Ruth Wilcox exists on two levels, the symbolic and the realistic. Symbolically, Ruth indeed represents a goal, an ideal of proportion and connection which Margaret attains in the course of the novel; but realistically, Ruth is just as impressed with Margaret's many virtues. Margaret's vivacity (*HE*, p. 10) and eloquence (*HE*, p. 73) keep the lonely and uprooted older woman from brooding, as she admits she is too apt to do (*HE*, p. 80).

Mrs. Wilcox gives Margaret a great gift, greater even than the gift of Howards End itself, for she shows Margaret how to care deeply for a place, for roots. Ruth's love for Howards End enables Margaret to accept the house itself. Margaret learns her lesson well and expects to end her life "caring most for a place" (*HE*, p. 130), but she must overcome great odds—indeed, the whole trend of modern life—to do so. When the Schlegels lose Wickham Place, they are "certainly the poorer for the loss. . . . It had helped to balance their lives, and almost to counsel them" (*HE*, p. 150). That they must move precisely nine months after they learn that the lease is about to expire (*HE*, p. 108) suggests a rebirth into a hostile, rootless modern world, and Margaret has great difficulty putting down roots elsewhere. When she is abruptly removed from Oniton after investing it with a great deal of emotion as her new home (*HE*, p. 249), she realizes that personal relations are suffering under a greater strain than ever before. They no longer receive any help from the earth in the flux of modern cosmopolitan life, for "the binding force that [trees and meadows and mountains] once exercised on character must be entrusted to Love alone. May Love be equal to the task!" (*HE*, p. 261). Ruth Wilcox's love for Henry, though great, is not equal to it; when she is separated from Howards End, she dies. Similarly, Margaret's love for Henry is most convincing when it is set in the natural world of Howards End, for only there does he connect.

Margaret's love for Henry has two aspects above and beyond her admiration for his competence at the outer life: she finds him physically appealing (*HE*, p. 132), and he is old enough to be her father, whom she respected. She sees love as a "central radiance" (*HE*, p. 165), something beyond sex which touches her personality (*HE*, p. 165). Margaret realizes that Henry does not mention love when he proposes (*HE*, p. 166), and she is willing to accept a nonexpressive love on his terms: "He must never be bothered with emotional talk, or with a display of sympathy. He was an elderly man now, and it would be futile and impudent to correct him" (*HE*, p. 166). She enters into marriage with her eyes open. She knows his faults (*HE*, p. 174), but "She loved him with too clear a vision to fear his cloudiness" (*HE*, p. 220).

One issue on which Henry is particularly cloudy and Margaret particularly clear-sighted is equality between the sexes. Margaret is identified with equality early in the novel when she (or poetry) is cited as Helen's source for the idea that equality is good (*HE*, p. 6). Later, in response to Mrs. Wilcox's antifeminism, Margaret explicitly articulates a feminism which is hardly radical:

Aren't we differing on something much wider [than the vote]? . . . Whether women are to remain what they have been since the dawn of history; or whether, since men have moved forward so far, they too may move forward a little now. I say they may.

[*HE*, pp. 77–78]

But a feminist Margaret in love with an antifeminist Henry does not find it easy to continue to move forward.

Henry is a charming antifeminist practically from the very first time we hear of him: Helen's second letter from Howards End states that Mr. Wilcox "says the most horrid things about women's suffrage so nicely" (*HE*, p. 5). On Chelsea Embankment he is protective, a trait which Helen resents but which Margaret accepts "as part of the good man's equipment" (*HE*, p. 130). Margaret finds his charm more impressive than his antifeminism, and she doesn't even mind his patronizing tone, because he is "old enough to be their father" (*HE*, p. 132). Henry considers the Schlegels clever but unpractical and suggests to his daughter Evie that "Until they marry, they ought to have someone to look after them" (*HE*, p. 148), a suggestion that reflects a rather different version of marriage from George Emerson's in *A Room with a View*.

Henry Wilcox, who refuses to take women seriously, believes that "women may say anything" (*HE*, p. 156); like Charles, he never really pays attention anyway. Ironically, he assumes that *women* do not pay attention, and in his business letter to Margaret about renting a house, "words were underlined, as is necessary when dealing with women" (*HE*, p. 157). Mr. Wilcox's idea of "an emancipated woman" (*HE*, p. 147) is adolescent and consists primarily of a woman to whom he can make smutty jokes and innuendoes, as we see when he misunderstands Leonard's walk. This is hardly Margaret's or Forster's idea of emancipation. And Henry no longer extends even this trivial aspect of "emancipation" to Margaret after they are engaged: "Now that she was going to marry him, he had grown particular. He discountenanced risqué conversation now" (*HE*, p. 231). Henry

condemns sexual language in women more strongly than illicit sexual action in men, as we see when he calls Margaret
indelicate for forthrightly asking if Jacky has been his
mistress (*HE,* p. 233). Henry *did* it; Margaret only *said* it,
but it is she whom he sees as indelicate.

Margaret's first attempt to challenge the Wilcox theories
of sexual roles and class barriers occurs during a motorcar
ride, after a train journey during which the arbitrary and
"chivalrous" distinctions of sexual roles are insisted on to
such an extent that "the long glass saloon . . . became a
forcing-house for the idea of sex" (*HE,* p. 210)—not, however, for *Margaret's* idea of sex. She tells Henry later, "You
men shouldn't be so chivalrous" (*HE,* p. 221), but when
asked "Why not?" answers untruthfully: "She knew why
not, but said that she did not know" (*HE,* p. 221). This second attempt to effect equality is as ineffective as her first,
when she jumps out of the moving car that has run over a
child's pet: "Why should the chauffeurs tackle the girl? Ladies sheltering behind men, men sheltering behind servants—the whole system's wrong, and she must challenge it"
(*HE,* p. 214). Unfortunately, she jumps too late to do any
good, but her action is a necessary reaction to an unreality
similar to that in *The Longest Journey,* for

she felt their whole journey from London had been unreal. They
had no part with the earth and its emotions. They were dust, and
a stink, and cosmopolitan chatter, and the girl whose cat had been
killed had lived more deeply then they.

[*HE,* p. 214]

Like Rickie Elliot, Margaret for a time succumbs to that
unreality. She negates her heroic jump by demeaning herself and telling Henry that she has been "naughty"
(*HE,* p. 214). We cannot take this change lightly, for earlier,
Margaret, with a clearer vision, "hated naughtiness more
than sin" (*HE,* p. 146). Margaret temporarily sells out to the
patronizing Wilcox views of "feminine nature" (*HE,* p. 215),

and the only "brotherhood" we see in *Howards End* is at the expense of women, when Margaret sees the wine-cellar at Oniton:

She, who kept all her wine at the bottom of the linen-cupboard, was astonished at the sight. "We shall never get through it!" she cried, and the two men were suddenly drawn into brotherhood, and exchanged smiles. She felt as if she had again jumped out of the car while it was moving.

[*HE*, p. 221]

Margaret admits to "kow-towing to the men" (*HE*, p. 223) to please Henry at Evie's wedding. Indeed, Evie's wedding marks the low point in their relationship. Her name, "Eve," reveals the fate that awaits Everywoman who does not strive for something beyond sexual stereotypes: Evie's personality, like her wedding, is utterly conventional. Margaret is unable to live up to the androgyny and equality of the wych-elm and lapses into the expected stereotyped role when she prepares Henry for her request that he help the Basts: "She was ashamed of her own diplomacy. In dealing with a Wilcox, how tempting it was to lapse from comradeship, and to give him the kind of woman that he desired!" (*HE*, p. 229). The situation is not hopeless, however, for although Margaret uses the conventional feminine devices of manipulation and influence, she knows that it is demeaning and wrong to do so:

Now she understood why some women prefer influence to rights. Mrs. Plynlimmon, when condemning suffragettes, had said: "The woman who can't influence her husband to vote the way she wants ought to be ashamed of herself." Margaret had winced, but she was influencing Henry now, and though pleased at her little victory, she knew that she had won it by the methods of the harem.

[*HE*, p. 230]

Margaret changes her loyalties in the course of the novel. At Evie's wedding, she defends her husband against her sis-

ter, but at the end she defends Helen against Henry [17] and
reasserts Schlegel values, ultimately convincing Henry of
their superiority. Sex makes the difference; Henry's attitude toward sexuality influences Margaret to change her
choice from Henry to Helen and eventually promote a reconciliation between them. Margaret can live with Henry's
failure to connect his own sexuality internally. But when he
condemns Helen for doing the same thing with Leonard
that he has done with Jacky, the lack of connection is too
great to bear, and Margaret finally stands up to him.

Henry's reaction to Jacky's reappearance is trite and conventional: "I am a man, and have lived a man's past"
(*HE,* p. 232). Margaret herself is still reacting according to
stereotypes: "She must not comment; comment is un-
feminine" (*HE,* p. 240). Henry can hardly believe that she
really forgives him and finally explains her forgiveness the
only way he can: "she was not altogether womanly. Her eyes
gazed too straight; they had read books that are suitable for
men only" (*HE,* p. 244). Henry is not entirely the conventional fool he seems, however, and he is not as insensitive as
most critics assume, for his choice of women is twice excellent, and on some level he is certainly *seeking* androgyny.
Consciously, however, he believes in the conventional
stereotypes which allow men to feel sexual temptation
but which assume that women are somehow immune
(*HE,* p. 245). Margaret almost accepts these stereotypes
when she is most disgusted at Henry and Jacky's affair (*HE,*
p. 240), but she soon regains her judgment and realizes that
the crucial variable is one of circumstances, not gender (*HE,*
p. 247). Her renewed faith in equality and comradeship
comes about through her own recognition that she finds a
handsome servant sexually attractive; as always, sexual
equality is linked to equality of class.

Margaret's reaction to Henry's "past," as to everything
else, is personal. Although she tries to feel that Henry's ac-

17. Howarth, Nov. 15, 1967.

tions had wronged her, she is unable to do so (*HE,* p. 243): "it was not her tragedy: it was Mrs. Wilcox's" (*HE,* p. 233). Margaret does not condemn the specifically sexual aspect of Henry's infidelity. What bothers her most is that he has betrayed another human being (*HE,* p. 246), a personal response of which he is incapable:

Unchastity and infidelity were as confused to him as to the Middle Ages, his only moral teacher. Ruth (poor old Ruth!) did not enter into his calculations at all, for poor old Ruth had never found him out.

[*HE,* p. 259]

Margaret's final judgment is tolerant, and her letter to Helen stresses "the need of charity in sexual matters: so little is known about them; it is hard enough for those who are personally touched to judge; then how futile must be the verdict of Society" (*HE,* p. 258). Margaret cannot yet understand the personal nature of Helen's answer, which thanks her for her "kind letter—rather a curious reply" (*HE,* pp. 258–59). Margaret does not find out until the end that her judgment of Henry and Jacky, or rather her tolerant refusal to judge them, applies equally to Helen and Leonard. As soon as she learns what Helen has done, she immediately extends to her sister the same tolerance she has given her husband. Henry's great fault is his inability to do the same, to connect.

Henry and Margaret's marriage runs smoothly for a time, entirely on Henry's terms: "He had only to call, and she clapped the book up and was ready to do what he wished" (*HE,* p. 259). She makes him a sandwich every morning and spends her time taking care of the house (*HE,* p. 262). Henry does not mind her cleverness, for "it distinguished her from the wives of other men," and he does not mind her spunk, for "as soon as he grew really serious, she gave in" (*HE,* p. 259). His view of sexual roles is archaic in the extreme: "Man is for war, woman for the recreation of the warrior, but he does not dislike it if she makes a show of fight. She cannot win in a real battle, having no muscles, only nerves" (*HE,* p. 259). His view ignores the personal, for we know that Margaret "had steady nerves" (*HE,* p. 177). When the real battle does come, the battle to connect, Margaret wins.

Margaret first begins to realize the necessity of reaffirming the Schlegel values of personal intercourse when Henry tries to leave without her to trap Helen at Howards End; and she realizes that

he was only treating her as she had treated Helen, and her rage at his dishonesty only helped to indicate what Helen would feel against them. She thought: "I deserve it: I am punished for lowering my colours."

[*HE,* p. 287]

To Henry, the female and the ill exist to be impersonally manipulated:

The sick had no rights; they were outside the pale; one could lie to them remorselessly. When his first wife was seized, he had promised to take her down to Hertfordshire, but meanwhile arranged with a nursing-home instead. Helen, too, was ill.

[*HE,* p. 283]

When Margaret sees the pregnant Helen, her Schlegel ideals triumph and she, unlike Henry, feels remorse at having treated Helen impersonally: "What would our father have thought of me?" (*HE,* p. 292). Henry's impersonal scheming becomes unbearable in the face of something as personal as a pregnancy, and Margaret sends him and the doctor away: "A new feeling came over her; she was fighting for women against men. She did not care about rights, but if men came into Howards End, it should be over her body" (*HE,* p. 290). Margaret asks Helen to forgive her (*HE,* p. 292), and the sisters find salvation in a common past: "They looked into each other's eyes. The inner life had paid" (*HE*, p. 299).

Margaret accepts Helen at this point, but her acceptance does not lead to a break with Henry until Henry himself refuses to accept Helen. Margaret remains a loyal wife and asks Henry's permission to allow Helen to stay overnight at Howards End (*HE*, p. 302), but he refuses and in addition asks for the name of Helen's "seducer," a word as hateful to Margaret as Charlotte's term "exploits" is to Lucy in *A Room with a View*. Margaret brilliantly stands up to Henry and tells him that he can't connect, that he's criminally muddled, that what Helen has done, he has done, and that both she and Mrs. Wilcox have spoiled him long enough (*HE*, p. 308).[18] Henry still does not give his permission for Helen to sleep in Howards End (*HE*, p. 309), but Margaret, who feels that she and Henry and Helen are all only fragments of Mrs. Wilcox's mind (*HE*, p. 313), stays there with her sister in spite of him. She decides to leave Henry and go to Germany with Helen, and she asks Charles to relay that message "with love" (*HE*, p. 327). Margaret never again falls away from the quest for the ideal of equality; she insists on comradeship or nothing. She recants nothing in her speech to Henry.

It was spoken not only to her husband, but to thousands of men like him—a protest against the inner darkness in high places that comes with a commercial age. . . . He had refused to connect, on the clearest issue that can be laid before a man, and their love must take the consequences.

[*HE*, p. 331]

Margaret seems to choose the fatherland when she decides to go to Germany, but her decision to stay overnight at

18. Gransden, *Forster*, p. 72, describes her speech as "one of the finest and deadliest pieces of feminism to have been written in the era of the suffragettes. How accurately Margaret diagnoses Henry's trouble: he has been spoilt. He inherited a man's world; he has always commanded; he has always been obeyed. When he took her out to lunch, he told her what to eat. Where it was his duty he considered other people's welfare, but never their feelings."

Howards End and her identification with Mrs. Wilcox are in effect a more solid choice of the motherland. Charles's murder of Leonard at Howards End reunites Margaret with Henry and leads to the final reconciliation, for Henry seems to realize that his own lack of connection has led to death. Immediately after the murder, Henry for the first time walks rather than motoring; Charles sees him as "more like a woman" (*HE,* pp. 328–29), but Henry is humanized rather than feminized. At the end of the novel, Margaret, Henry, Helen, and Helen's baby are all living at Howards End, motherland and fatherland are united, and the Schlegel ideals are established in the English countryside.

Howards End itself is practically a character in the novel as well as its main symbol. To the Wilcoxes, it is merely a house, and they do not know that to Ruth Howard Wilcox "it had been a spirit, for which she sought a spiritual heir" (*HE,* p. 98). Forster's "commentator" does not at first condemn the Wilcoxes for ignoring Mrs. Wilcox's last request, that the house go to Margaret (*HE,* p. 98), but neither does he ultimately exonerate them:

The practical moralist may acquit them absolutely. He who strives to look deeper may acquit them—almost. For one hard fact remains. They did neglect a personal appeal. The woman who had died did say to them: "Do this," and they answered: "We will not."
[*HE,* p. 99]

He poses the question of the very existence of spiritual heredity:

Is it credible that the possessions of the spirit can be bequeathed at all? Has the soul offspring? A wych-elm tree, a vine, a wisp of hay with dew on it—can passion for such things be transmitted where there is no bond of blood?
[*HE,* pp. 98–99]

If there is spiritual heredity, then physical heredity assumes less importance. Margaret Schlegel, Forster's greatest character, is physically barren, but her barrenness does not imply an emotional or intellectual sterility, and Forster in fact refers specifically to her "fertility" (*HE*, p. 183). Physical fertility is clearly not the most important thing in *Howards End,* for Charles and Dolly Wilcox "breed like rabbits" (*HE*, p. 274) but are certainly not to be more admired than Margaret. Margaret's barrenness unites her with Maurice, who is necessarily barren because of his homosexuality. This parallel suggests that sensitive and intellectual people, especially women, may also share other problems with homosexuals.

Howards End itself is fertile, and its nine rooms suggest the nine months of gestation; Helen's child is born in the central room of the nine (*HE*, p. 339). Early in the novel, Margaret sees houses as either masculine or feminine (*HE*, p. 44), and two years after Ruth's death Henry rejects Howards End because "it is neither one thing nor the other. One must have one thing or the other" (*HE*, p. 136). But Howards End is androgynous,[19] like its wych-elm, and at the end of the novel it connects all sexes and all classes in the Schlegels, Wilcoxes, and Basts:

In these English farms, if anywhere, one might see life steadily and see it whole, group in one vision its transitoriness and its eternal youth, connect—connect without bitterness until all men are brothers.

[*HE*, p. 269]

And until all women are sisters and all people androgynous siblings.

When Margaret first sees Howards End, she is impressed with the fertility of its soil and decides that the place is beautiful. Not surprisingly, the door to the androgynous Howards End is not locked to an androgynous Margaret, although Henry is off somewhere busily trying to find the key

19. Crews, *Perils of Humanism,* p. 112, infers that "The house apparently stands for the integrated family life that was led there by Ruth Wilcox and is to be continued by Margaret."

(*HE,* p. 200). It opens to those who love it; and after a moment's hesitation, she goes in without waiting for Henry. Howards End returns to Margaret the sense of space the motorcar has taken away (*HE,* p. 201), and once inside, she is greeted by Miss Avery, an "old maid" (*HE,* p. 202) with spiritual fertility, "the sibylline character who cares for the house." [20] Miss Avery really does "care for" Howards End, and she greets Margaret as Ruth Wilcox's spiritual successor. Margaret is shocked when Miss Avery confuses her with Mrs. Wilcox and stammers, "I—Mrs. Wilcox—I?" (*HE,* p. 202) as if she cannot quite believe it, but that will indeed be her name when she marries Henry. Margaret loves England for the first time "through the house and old Miss Avery" (*HE,* p. 204), and she loves Henry for having saved it (*HE,* p. 205).

Miss Avery herself could have owned Howards End if she had married Ruth's brother or uncle Tom, who proposed to her, but unlike Margaret, she chose not to marry, and Tom Howard died (*HE,* p. 203). The name "Howards End" implies the end of the Howards, and Miss Avery tells Margaret that "Things went on until there were no men" (*HE,* p. 274). Margaret corrects her by adding, "Until Mr. Wilcox came along," a statement Miss Avery accepts with qualification: "Wilcoxes are better than nothing, as I see you've found" (*HE,* p. 274). Dolly implies that Miss Avery was responsible for Tom Howard's death and thus for the Howards' end; but the unmentioned corollary to this fact is that Ruth, obviously the spiritual owner of Howards End, can become the legal owner only by the death of her brother, for men inherit before women, just as Tibby gets more money than Margaret or Helen (*HE,* p. 61). The desire for physical heredity, while not of primary importance in *Howards End,* could still be fulfilled more easily if women were considered people. A family physically dies out, or ends, when its last member dies, not when its last man does.

20. Trilling, *Forster,* p. 133.

The end of the Howards comes about because women must change their names when they marry, and Ruth Howard becomes Ruth Wilcox.

If Miss Avery is the heart of Howards End, as she seems to be, and if Howards End is England,[21] then its heart is feminine, but its body is disfigured because of a false idea of femininity. The beams in the dining room and hall are open, but the drawing room's beam is match-boarded— "Because the facts of life must be concealed from ladies?" (*HE*, p. 200). Margaret, inside Howards End with Helen near the end of the novel, calls it "a room that men have spoilt through trying to make it nice for women. Men don't know what we want—" (*HE*, pp. 297–98). Helen adds, "And never will," but Margaret is more optimistic: "In two thousand years they'll know" (*HE*, p. 298).

Miss Avery, who moves the Schlegel furniture and books into Howards End against Mr. Wilcox's express orders, asserts to Margaret, "The house has been empty long enough" (*HE*, p. 271). Miss Avery, the heart of Howards End, puts Mr. Schlegel's sword within easy reach of Charles, who kills Leonard with it, implying that the house itself has "heart disease" from being empty. Miss Avery informs Margaret that she is fated to live there, that, in fact, she is already living there (*HE*, p. 272), for she loves it. Margaret is forced to admit that "the furniture fitted extraordinarily well" (*HE*, p. 273).[22] Howards End wakes up the Schlegel furniture, which never got any sun at Wickham Place (*HE*, p. 300), and the house itself comes alive with Schlegel furniture and Schlegel women in it. Miss Avery puts Tibby's old bassinette in Helen's old room (*HE*, p. 273); she seems to know about Helen's pregnancy without being told, just as Ruth Wilcox had known about Helen and Paul's love. Helen recognizes immediately that Howards End is a Schlegel

---

21. Ibid., p. 118.
22. Trilling, ibid., p. 133, points out that "by the agency of women, the best of traditional England is furnished with the stuff of the intellect."

house: "We know this is our house, because it feels ours. Oh, they may take the title-deeds and the doorkeys, but for this one night we are at home" (*HE*, p. 302).

At the end of the novel, Henry Wilcox's will finally corresponds with Ruth's, for he also leaves Margaret Howards End:

> "Then I leave Howards End to my wife absolutely." . . .
> Margaret did not answer. There was something uncanny in her triumph. She, who had never expected to conquer anyone, had charged straight through these Wilcoxes and broken up their lives.
>
> [*HE*, p. 341]

Henry leaves Margaret no money by her own wish; she has prevailed upon him to be generous rather than just to his children, and "She intends to diminish her income by half during the next ten years" (*HE*, p. 341). In the next generation Howards End will go to Helen's child, a symbolic acceptance of the sexual union of the classes. Margaret and Henry's marriage at Howards End reflects what Margaret has called "the comradeship, not passionate, that is our highest gift as a nation" (*HE*, p. 268), and it fulfills the vision Margaret had the first time she saw the house and its symbolic wych-elm:

> It was a comrade. House and tree transcended any similes of sex.
> . . . Yet they kept within limits of the human. Their message was not of eternity, but of hope on this side of the grave. As she stood in the one, gazing at the other, truer relationship had gleamed.
>
> [*HE*, p. 206]

Five
A Passage to India

Imperialism pervades this novel. Against a background of oppression and manipulation of Indians by their British rulers, a parallel domestic imperialism emerges: Indian men oppress their women, while British women manipulate their men.[1]

These manipulative British women are one of the chief obstacles to friendship between the races in India, as Forster dramatically asserts at the Bridge Party ostensibly arranged to promote such friendship: "The Englishmen had intended to play up better, but had been prevented from doing so by their women folk, whom they had to attend, provide with tea, advise about dogs, etc." [2] Cyril Fielding, the male protagonist [3] and virtually the only English man in the novel to attempt to bridge the races through friendship, is rejected early by the wives of his colleagues as "not a sahib

1. The contrasting cultures in *Where Angels Fear to Tread* reveal a similar contrast between Italian and English.

2. E. M. Forster, *A Passage to India* (New York: Harcourt, Brace, 1924), p. 46. All future references to this work will appear in the text in the abbreviated form *P*. The more readily available Harvest paperback edition follows the same pagination, as does the Modern Library edition.

These women remind us of Mrs. Failing in *The Longest Journey*, who exhibits a similar disinclination to bridge gulfs. Trilling, *Forster*, pp. 48–49, notes this connection when he refers to Mrs. Failing as one of "Forster's sadistic women." He continues: "The type will be institutionalized in *A Passage to India* in the wives of the English officials who regard the Indians with a vindictive cruelty which is usually absent from their husbands' feeling and which is said to constitute one of the major emotional difficulties of administration."

3. Like *Where Angels Fear to Tread*, *A Passage to India* has two protagonists, one male and one female: Cyril Fielding and Adela Quested.

really" (*P*, p. 64) because he refuses to play the expected role. He is not "lively and helpful," and he "never advised one about dogs or horses, or dined, or paid his midday calls, or decorated trees for one's children at Christmas" (*P*, pp. 62–63).

The Anglo-Indian women, who in this manner attempt to manipulate their own men, treat Indians dreadfully. As the Indians in the novel realize, and Hamidullah articulates, "They all become exactly the same, not worse, not better. I give any Englishman two years. . . . And I give any Englishwoman six months" (*P*, p. 11).[4] Adela Quested is considered odd because she wants to see Indians (*P*, p. 26); the standard British female attitude is represented by the nurse who asserts that "One's only hope was to hold sternly aloof," and by Mrs. Callendar, who believes that "the kindest thing one can do to a native is to let him die" (*P*, p. 27). This cruel insistence on caste distinctions probably occurs because Anglo-Indian women have no work or interests of their own—they "did nothing that they could not share with the men" (*P*, p. 40)—and thus they focus all their energies into manipulating their own men and being rude to Indians. Themselves considered inferior to Anglo-Indian men, they feel that they must be superior to someone; and the Indians, a subject race, are pathetically available.

Mrs. Turton, wife of the Collector, the ranking British official in Chandrapore, epitomizes the worst of Anglo-Indian womanhood. Not surprisingly, she dislikes Adela and identifies her with Fielding: she finds them both not "pukka" (*P*, p. 28), or genuine. Mrs. Turton, by contrast, is genuinely awful, and Mahmoud Ali ironically points out that she is worse than the natives: "When we poor blacks take bribes, we perform what we are bribed to perform, and the law discovers us in consequence. The English take and do nothing.

---

4. Trilling, *Forster*, p. 149, asserts that "of all the English it is the women who insist most strongly on their superiority, who are the rawest and the crudest in their manner."

I admire them" (*P,* p. 11). Like Mrs. Failing, Mrs. Turton feels no unity with other women. She despises Indian women even more than she does Indian men, and when they come to the Bridge Party, she is dismayed: "Oh, those purdah women!" (*P,* p. 41). She cannot communicate socially with the Indian women, for "She had learnt the lingo, but only to speak to her servants, so she knew none of the politer forms and of the verbs only the imperative mood" (*P,* p. 42). She is hardly equipped for a Bridge Party, and her advice to Adela and Mrs. Moore bears out her snobbery and racial prejudice: "You're superior to them, anyway. Don't forget that. You're superior to everyone in India except one or two of the Ranis, and they're on an equality" (*P,* pp. 41–42). Mrs. Turton exhibits what Margaret Schlegel in *Howards End* calls the "tragedy of preparedness" (*HE,* p. 107), but since Mrs. Turton is hardly capable of tragedy, the effect is ironic: "She was 'saving herself up,' as she called it . . . for some vague future occasion when a high official might come along and tax her social strength" (*P,* p. 39).

What does happen to make Mrs. Turton let herself go is Adela's charge of rape against Aziz, an event which looses a storm of cliché on the Anglo-Indian community. The hysterical reaction against all Indians is begun by Mr. Turton, his wife's counterpart, whose twenty-five stale and ungenerous years in India have taught him only that social bridges are impossible (*P,* p. 164). He speaks in impersonal jargon which has nothing to do with either Adela or Aziz: "That a lady, that a young lady engaged to my most valued subordinate—that she—an English girl fresh from England—" (*P,* pp. 164–65). Fielding reveals his heroism at this point, for his reaction is personal: "He had not gone mad at the phrase 'an English girl fresh from England,' he had not rallied to the banner of race. He was still after facts, though the herd had decided on emotion" (*P,* p. 165). Mr. Turton's reaction prevails at the British club, where "they

had started speaking of 'women and children'—that phrase
that exempts the male from sanity when it has been repeated a few times" (*P*, p. 183). Misguided chivalry here is
as destructive on a racial level as it has been on a personal
level in Forster's other novels. No one treats Adela as a person: the men are too respectful, the women too sympathetic
(*P*, p. 193).

Forster ironically states that "Although Miss Quested had
not made herself popular with the English, she brought out
all that was fine in their character" (*P*, p. 179). "All that was
fine" turns out to be an "exalted emotion" (*P*, p. 179) of sisterhood which is almost a parody of the sisterhood in *Howards End*, for here the main point is to exclude everyone
who isn't British: "By the side of their compassionate love
for Adela another sentiment sprang up which was to stran-
gle it in the long run" (*P*, p. 182), an anti-Indian chauvin-
ism. Adela is soon replaced as the focal point of the furor,
for she is not pretty enough, and significantly a beautiful,
brainless young mother takes her place as the symbol of
British womanhood: "with her abundant figure and masses
of corn-gold hair, she symbolized all that is worth fighting
and dying for; more permanent a symbol, perhaps, than
poor Adela" (*P*, p. 181). Despite her low social status, this
woman so impresses Mrs. Turton that the older woman
vows "not to be such a snob" (*P*, p. 181)—among Anglo-
Indians, of course.

The day of Aziz's trial, chivalry is revealed as inadequate
for both men and women. Mr. Turton resents Adela and
blames women for British difficulties in India; Forster
suggests that "perhaps there is a grain of resentment in all
chivalry" (*P*, p. 214). Mrs. Turton's pent-up frustration expresses itself in an accusation that the British men are
"weak, weak, weak," for she wants, not justice, but revenge
against Indians: "Why, they ought to crawl from here to the
caves on their hands and knees whenever an Englishwoman's in sight" (*P*, p. 216). When Adela recants, Mrs.

Turton becomes hysterical and calls for the prosecution to continue anyway: "Call the other witnesses; we're none of us safe" (*P*, p. 130). As before, but more clearly, her hatred has nothing to do with fact.

Muslim women don't exist to the British; the hunger strike several of them go on until Aziz is acquitted is ineffective, because "their death would make little difference, indeed, being invisible, they seemed dead already" (*P*, p. 214). Indian women barely exist to their fellow Indians; they live behind the purdah (*P*, p. 13) in a state of oppression greater even than that of Italian wives in *Where Angels Fear to Tread*. We do not see much of Indian women in *A Passage to India*, but the one glimpse we do get behind the purdah, when Aziz is talking to his aunt, Hamidullah Begum, is disquieting: "It was difficult to get away, because until they had had their dinner she would not begin hers, and consequently prolonged her remarks" (*P*, p. 13).

Woman's only role is to be married; Indian society allows her nothing else:

better polygamy almost, than that a woman should die without the joys God has intended her to receive. Wedlock, motherhood, power in the house—for what else is she born, and how can the man who has denied them to her stand up to face her creator and his own at the last day?

[*P*, p. 14]

Men marry only because they see it as their duty to save women from the "tragedy" of an unwed life (*P*, p. 14) and in order to have children; as in Italy, women barely exist in their own right.

Aziz's marriage is the only one we are told about in any depth, and it begins in the traditional manner, arranged by others. His wife loves him, and he falls in love with her also, shortly before she dies giving him a second son (*P*, p. 55). Aziz's attitude toward his children defines the position of women in India: when he lists his children to Mrs. Moore, he lists the girl last although she is the oldest (*P*, p. 22). His daughter counts for nothing; when Aziz is sick and sleeping, he entertains happy memories of "his honoured wife and dear boys" (*P*, p. 122). Like Lilia in *Where Angels Fear to Tread*, Indian women exist to bear sons.

Near the end of *A Passage to India*, Hamidullah wants his wife to come out of purdah, but she refuses, and will not even see Fielding, a close friend (*P*, p. 271); she has internalized purdah. The feeling of nonexistence is difficult to overcome all at once, and the only hope for the future lies in the young: only if Aziz can see his daughter as a person will purdah be effectively lifted in India. And the lifting of purdah is not merely an Indian problem; western women can be just as invisible behind a veil of "ladylikeness."

At the very end of the novel, Aziz's "poems were all on one topic—Oriental womanhood" (*P*, p. 293), and they all had the theme that the purdah must go. He declares that women as well as men must fight the invaders, a notion which Forster finds fantastic (*P*, p. 293) but which today does not seem so farfetched if one looks at modern Israel. Aziz strikes what Forster calls a true note, that "there cannot be a motherland without new homes" (*P*, p. 293), but Fielding points out that Aziz does not himself create a new home: "Free your own lady in the first place, and see who'll wash Ahmad, Karim, and Jemila's faces. A nice situation!" (*P*, p. 321). What neither Fielding nor Aziz realizes is that as long as Jemila comes last on that list, no one is free.

Love and friendship are parallel in *A Passage to India*. Aziz feels that his wife can never be replaced: "a friend would come nearer to her than another woman" (*P*, p. 55). At this point in the novel, Aziz believes in the purdah, but he shows his wife to his brothers: "All men are my brothers, and as soon as one behaves as such he may see my wife" (*P*, p. 116). This is a bit more humane than the system in Italy, where *caffè* brotherhood is strictly segregated from domestic life. Fielding's comment on being shown the photograph of Aziz's wife implies a solution to India's "woman problem" which would work equally well in Italy, England, or anywhere: "And when the whole world behaves as such, there will be no more purdah?" (*P,* p. 116). At the end of the novel, although universal brotherhood seems impossible, Fielding does make the one personal gesture essential to friendship and "forced himself to speak intimately about his wife, the person most dear to him" (*P,* p. 319).

Aziz, as the recipient of much of the snobbery in the novel, is extremely sensitive about the rights and feelings of the oppressed race to which he belongs, but he never connects and feels sympathy for women, a similarly oppressed group. He especially feels no concern for unbeautiful women; like Gino Carella in *Where Angels Fear to Tread,* he is a sexual snob. Aziz is particularly enraged to be accused of sexual assault "by a woman who had no personal beauty" (*P,* p. 241). Fielding recognizes this attitude for what it is and in doing so wins our admiration:

It was, in a new form, the old, old trouble that eats the heart out of every civilization: snobbery, the desire for possessions, creditable appendages; and it is to escape this rather than the lusts of the flesh that saints retreat into the Himalayas.

[*P,* p. 241]

Fielding, who views women as people, becomes very upset at the letter of apology Aziz wants Adela to write: "Dear Dr. Aziz, I wish you had come into the cave; I am an awful old hag, and it is my last chance" (*P,* p. 253). Their differing views of women are a major source of disagreement between Aziz and Fielding and a significant reason for considering Fielding rather than Aziz the hero of the novel.

The one woman in the novel to whom Aziz does not condescend sexually is Mrs. Moore, whom he worships; significantly, he meets her in a mosque. Although at first he assumes that she is merely another Mrs. Turton and yells at

her that she has no right to be there and should have taken
off her shoes, she soon wins him over completely by announcing that she has already done so. He is charmed, and
in consequence differentiates her from other women: "so
few ladies take the trouble, especially if thinking no one is
there to see" (*P,* p. 20). Mrs. Moore's answer, "God is here"
(*P,* p. 20), impresses us, as it does Aziz, with its simplicity
and sensitivity. Mrs. Moore, honest and straightforward in
her judgment of her fellow countrywomen, does not accept
Aziz's hypocritical remark that Mrs. Callendar is "A very
charming lady" (*P,* p. 22) and qualifies it in her response:
"Possibly, when one knows her better" (*P,* p. 22). This will-
ingness to criticize a member of the ruling caste elicits from
Aziz a burst of feeling, for he has just been snubbed by Mrs.
Callendar, and henceforth he sees Mrs. Moore as his ally
against the forces of oppression (*P,* p. 23). He tells her that
she understands him, a comment which surprises her, and
her answer, "I don't think I understand people very well. I
only know whether I like or dislike them" (*P,* p. 23), proves
to Aziz that she is an oriental. Mrs. Moore is thus the only
woman in the novel truly to bridge the races. The only
other person to do likewise is her son Ralph, on whom Aziz
passes the same judgment at the end of the book
(*P,* p. 311). Aziz, who looks down on women, can worship
Mrs. Moore because her womanhood is not the primary factor of her existence. She is a person, and her identification
with her son in the act of connecting and bridging cultures
suggests a corresponding bridge over arbitrary sexual differences: both Mrs. Moore and Ralph are androgynous.
Mrs. Moore has the added factor of age, and Aziz is surprised to see that she has "a red face and white hair"
(*P,* p. 20), for her voice is young; his attitude changes accordingly. An elderly woman is more easily considered a
person, for her age takes her out of the sexual arena, and
Mrs. Moore has as much in common with Mr. Emerson of *A
Room with a View* as she does with Mrs. Wilcox of *Howards*

End. Most critics see Mrs. Moore as a "great mother" figure,[5] and this is not particularly harmful if we keep in mind Forster's androgynous Demeter.

Unfortunately Ronny, Mrs. Moore's philistine son, sees his mother not as an androgynous "great mother" but merely as "the mater" (*P*, p. 29), as Charles Wilcox sees Ruth in *Howards End*. Ronny limits her to her societal role and never appreciates any of her transcendent qualities, just as he limits Indians to their role as inferior beings and never appreciates their humanity. He insensitively attributes his mother's religious temperament to "bad health" and "ageing" (*P*, p. 52). Mrs. Moore defends Aziz to Ronny, declaring that he is her "real friend" (*P*, p. 97), and indeed "Mrs. Moore finds a truer son than Ronny in Dr. Aziz." [6]

Mrs. Moore notices "how tolerant and conventional [Ronny's] judgments had become" (*P*, p. 40), but his tolerance, as his mother realizes, is not of other human beings, of Indians, but of mediocrity in things British; it parallels Mrs. Turton's incipient lack of snobbery toward the pretty young Englishwoman. Ronny is impersonal, and when Mrs. Moore tells him that Adela is upset over the treatment of Indians, his outburst is directed at all women, not just Adela: "Oh, how like a woman to worry over a side-issue!" (*P*, p. 49). He angrily asserts, "We're not out here for the purpose of behaving pleasantly! . . . We're out here to do justice and keep the peace" (*P*, pp. 49–50). Mrs. Moore, who can identify with other women and with Indians, not to mention wasps, tells him that his "sentiments are those of a god" (*P*, p. 50), and she is even more upset at his manner: "One touch of regret—not the canny substitute but the true regret from the heart—would have made him a different man, and the British Empire a different institution" (*P*, p. 51). Her answer asserts her belief in personal relations, the highest good in *Howards End;* she believes that "The English *are* out here to be pleasant" (*P*, p. 51): "Be-

5. For example, McDowell, *Forster*, p. 124.   6. Trilling, *Forster*, p. 100.

cause India is part of the earth. And God has put us on the earth in order to be pleasant to each other. God . . . is . . . love" (Forster's ellipses; *P,* p. 51).

Mrs. Moore's religion of the sanctity of personal relations is not satisfactory in the world view of *A Passage to India,* as it is in *Howards End.* Mrs. Moore is telepathic, like Mrs. Wilcox; but while what is known without words in *Howards End* is love, in *A Passage to India* it is the "ghost" or hyena on the road (*P,* p. 97), another image for the evil in the caves.[7] Mrs. Moore begins to be dissatisfied with her God as soon as she enters India (*P,* p. 52), and her experience in the Marabar Caves marks her total disillusionment. The message of the caves, that "Everything exists, nothing has value," begins, in the form of an echo, "to undermine her hold on life" (*P,* p. 149), and she loses all interest in personal relations and everything else. She loses the desire to communicate with anyone, even God (*P,* p. 150), and succumbs to apathy (*P,* p. 158); she loses her "Christian tenderness" and exhibits "a just irritation against the human race" (*P,* p. 199). She does not visit Adela, although she is the only visitor Adela wants. The only part of Adela's situation that interests her is the echo (*P,* p. 200). She exists in a "spiritual muddledom" (*P,* p. 208):

She had come to that state where the horror of the universe and its smallness are both visible at the same time—the twilight of the double vision in which so many elderly people are involved.

[*P,* p. 207]

Only on her way home does she realize that the Marabar is only one of many Indias, that it is not the final answer (*P,* p. 210); but her realization comes too late to save her life, and she dies at sea (*P,* pp. 246–47). Her death is not final either, any more than is Mrs. Wilcox's, and Mrs. Moore continues after death as "Esmiss Esmoor, a Hindu

7. Howarth, Nov. 22, 1967.

goddess" (*P*, p. 225). Although she cannot incorporate Hinduism, Hinduism incorporates her, and we too are left with
a "double vision," of despair and hope.

Mrs. Moore's experience in the cave drastically changes
her interest in love from specifically Christian and married
love to the belief that all love is the same. She begins the
novel wondering whether Adela and Ronny's engagement
will work out, for she sees such concerns as her role in life:
"She was past marrying herself, even unhappily; her function was to help others, her reward to be informed that she
was sympathetic. Elderly ladies must not expect more than
this" (*P*, p. 95). She herself has had two happy marriages
and believes in that institution: "excellent it was to see the
incident repeated by the younger generation" (*P*, p. 95).
She believes, like Jacky Bast, that "marriage makes most
things right enough" (*P*, p. 98), even though we see clearly
that there is no love between Adela and Ronny. Her attitude toward marriage and children is rather conventional,
and unfortunately it convinces Adela:

It is the children who are the first consideration. Until they are
grown up and married off. When that happens one has again the
right to live for oneself—in the plains or the hills, as suits.

[*P*, pp. 134–35]

Her argument does not convince us, especially if we remember the lesson of Mrs. Elliot in *The Longest Journey,* who
lived only for others.

After Mrs. Moore emerges from the caves, she no longer
believes in personal relations or marriage:

She felt increasingly (vision or nightmare?) that, though people
are important, the relations between them are not, and that in
particular too much fuss has been made over marriage; centuries
of carnal embracement, yet man is no nearer to understanding
man.

[*P*, p. 135]

Marriage seems futile: "Why all this marriage, marriage? . . . The human race would have become a single person centuries ago if marriage was any use" (*P*, pp. 201–2). Even rape seems just another form of love: "love in a church, love in a cave, as if there is the least difference" (*P*, p. 202). Mrs. Moore knows that nothing happened in the cave but asserts that even "if it had, there are worse evils than love" (*P*, p. 208).

In the end, Aziz wonders, as we do, just why the final impression of Mrs. Moore is so positive:

What did this eternal goodness of Mrs. Moore amount to? To nothing, if brought to the test of thought. She had not borne witness in his favour, nor visited him in the prison, yet she had stolen to the depths of his heart, and he always adored her.

[*P*, p. 312]

He never knows, and neither do we, but because of her influence he is finally able to recognize Adela's heroism, forgive her, and write her that he would always connect her with the name of Mrs. Moore, "the name that is very sacred in my mind" (*P*, p. 320).

Adela Quested is the female protagonist of the novel. Her name implies a search or quest, and she comes to India looking for "the *real* India" (*P*, p. 24) and for marriage; she finds instead real Indians, sexuality, and self-knowledge. She is a cross between Caroline Abbott and Harriet Herriton of *Where Angels Fear to Tread*. Like Caroline, she discovers her own sexuality but is unable to fulfill it; like Harriet, she resists her environment. Adela resents the apathy that India, and Professor Godbole's song in particular, instill in her (*P*, p. 133) as Harriet resents the gaiety of the Italian opera.

Adela gains our sympathy by "her rather dull decency." [8] She is distressed that the Bridge Party is a failure and angry

8. Trilling, *Forster*, p. 145.

at the Anglo-Indian community for "inviting guests and not treating them properly!" (*P*, p. 46). Yet her liberalism, merely intellectual, does not touch her emotions. Although she insists that she herself not be labeled and informs Fielding that she dislikes mysteries "not because I'm English, but from my own personal point of view" (*P*, p. 69), she does not extend Aziz the same privilege: "She regarded him as 'India,' and never surmised that his outlook was limited and his method inaccurate, and that no one is India" (*P*, p. 72).

We are first introduced to Adela in conjunction with Ronny (*P*, p. 24), a fact which colors our impression of her throughout the novel. Before the incident at the caves, the primary suspense of the novel hinges on whether or not Adela will marry him, and since we like Adela and dislike Ronny, we hope not. Adela and Ronny were originally attracted to each other because of a shared belief in "the sanctity of personal relationships" (*P*, p. 84), but Ronny has become official (*P*, pp. 80–81), and we are surprised that she even considers going through with the marriage. When she breaks the engagement the first time, Forster stresses their similarity: "Experiences, not character, divided them; they were not dissimilar, as humans go" (*P*, p. 85). Ronny decently accepts her refusal; he is at his best in renunciation, like Cecil Vyse. We are glad when Adela breaks her engagement, not because we prefer celibacy to marriage— the reason Mr. Beebe rejoices when Lucy breaks her engagement in *A Room with a View* (*R*, p. 219)—but because the vision of Adela's projected married life is so ghastly: centering around the club, their life will consist of entertaining and being entertained by Turtons and Burtons (*P*, p. 47).

Only when Adela spontaneously tells Aziz that she does not plan to stay in India (*P*, p. 73) does she realize, for the first time, that she has no desire to marry Ronny, but she is very upset at her behavior (*P*, pp. 81–82) and later changes her mind again. If she had followed her inner promptings, the catastrophe might have been avoided, but ironically Adela, who insists on living a totally intellectualized life, makes the same mistake as the flighty Lilia in *Where Angels Fear to Tread* and convinces herself that superficial sexuality is love.

Adela renews her engagement after a car accident which literally throws her together with Ronny. They touch hands, experience an animal thrill; and "a spurious unity descended on them" (*P*, p. 88). Adela refers later to "The animal thing that hit us" (*P*, p. 98),[9] and the "animal thing" is Adela's repressed sexuality, for after the accident, "Adela in her excitement knelt and swept her skirts about, until it was she if anyone who appeared to have attacked the car" (*P*, p. 90). When Adela renews her engagement, she wishes that there had been a dramatic scene between herself and Ronny, but she experiences no release and feels especially constrained because she is now labeled (*P*, p. 94).

The imagery surrounding the expedition to the caves suggests her sexual, repressed frame of mind. At first the description of the expedition seems to predict Adela and Ronny's forthcoming marriage: "no one was enthusiastic, yet it took place" (*P*, p. 127). The disappointing sunrise on the day of the trip is explicitly sexual: "Why, when the chamber was prepared, did the bridegroom not enter with trumpets and shawms, as humanity expects? The sun rose without splendour" (*P*, p. 137). Adela imagines that she sees a snake (*P*, pp. 140–41), but realizes on closer inspection with field glasses that it is merely a tree stump; if indeed "the snake must be regarded as a phallic symbol," then "the little episode heralds the catastrophic delusion which will occur further on."[10] The caves themselves continue the

9. Martial Rose, *Literature in Perspective*, p. 81, says she "realizes that her engagement is based merely on an animal impulse."

10. Keith Hollingsworth, "*A Passage to India:* The Echoes in the Marabar Caves" in *Perspectives on E. M. Forster's* A Passage to India: *A Collection of Critical Essays*, ed. V. A. Shahane (New York, Barnes and Noble, 1968), p. 46.

sexual imagery, for they are uterine, resembling the root of all life: [11] when Aziz takes offense at Adela's question about polygamy, he "plunged into" (*P*, p. 153) a cave. [12]

Before that fatal question, Adela offends Aziz by advocating a universal something to break down barriers: [13] "She was only recommending the universal brotherhood [Aziz] sometimes dreamed of, but as soon as it was put into prose it became untrue" (*P*, p. 145). Adela's central problem is that she is totally prosaic and, unlike Margaret Schlegel, cannot unite prose and passion.

As Adela enters the caves, she thinks, "What about love? . . . She and Ronny—no, they did not love each other" (*P*, p. 152). She does not "connect" with Ronny: "There was esteem and animal contact at dusk, but the emotion that linked them was absent" (*P*, p. 152). She is "vexed" but not "appalled" by her realization. She does not want to break off the engagement, partly because she does not want to cause trouble and partly because "She wasn't convinced that love is necessary to a successful union" (*P*, p. 152). This is a "Forsterian heresy," [14] and Adela commits a second heresy when she tries to get her emotions "well under control" (*P*, p. 152). Some release seems inevitable, and as she enters the cave she is thinking sexually about Aziz (*P*, p. 153). On some level, Adela no longer wants to see things coldly and

11. Howarth, Nov. 22, 1967.

12. The sexual imagery that leads up to Adela's sexual hallucination leads down from it also, as Louise Dauner, "What Happened in the Cave? Reflections on *A Passage to India*," in Shahane, *Perspectives,* p. 58, points out: "It is not exaggerated perhaps to see some phallic symbolism in the penetration of the cactus-needles, a delicate irony."

13. Immediately before entering the caves, Adela asks Aziz's advice on how to avoid becoming a typical Anglo-Indian (*P*, p. 146), and Gertrude M. White, "*A Passage to India:* Analysis and Revaluation," in *Twentieth Century Interpretations of* A Passage to India: *A Collection of Critical Essays,* ed. Andrew Rutherford (Englewood Cliffs, N. J., Prentice-Hall, Inc., 1970), p. 59, sees a clear analogy "between the personal situation of Adela and Ronny" and "the political situation between India and England." Interestingly, she sees Adela's relationship with Ronny, not with Aziz, as the central rape in the novel, as union without love.

14. Crews, *Perils of Humanism,* p. 159.

intellectually, and the caves give her a needed emotional release.[15] She cannot yet accept the reality of her own sexuality, however, and instead destructively blames Aziz for a sexual desire she later realizes is internal. Mr. Turton describes the incident in the cave to Fielding in terms which remind us of George Emerson's kiss in *A Room with a View:* "Miss Quested has been insulted in one of the Marabar caves" (*P,* p. 163). Sex, even imaginary sex, is still considered an insult.

After her hallucination, Adela alternates between logic and hysteria (*P,* p. 194). She feels "that it was her crime" (*P,* p. 194), but the "it" has indefinite reference, and we do not know if on some level she realizes that she has had a hallucination, or rather if she realizes that "her crime" was not loving Ronny. The influence of Mrs. Moore makes Adela doubt her story (*P,* p. 202), but at this point she is "neurotic" (*P,* p. 204) to the extent that she will believe anything anybody tells her and is equally receptive to the assumption of the Anglo-Indian community that Aziz is guilty.

Adela's main neurotic symptom is her echo, which temporarily disappears when she tells Mrs. Moore that Aziz is innocent.[16] All the women in the book are linked to an echo: Mrs. Moore hears one after *her* experience in the caves; at the Bridge Party there is no communication between Adela and the purdah women because of "the echoing walls of their civility" (*P,* p. 43); and an echo links Adela and Aziz's wife.[17]

15. Ted E. Boyle, "Adela Quested's Delusion: The Failure of Rationalism in *A Passage to India*" in Shahane, *Perspectives,* p. 74, suggests that as Adela enters the cave, she thinks with half her mind that sight-seeing bores her, and wonders "with the other half about marriage" (*P,* p. 153); inside the caves, her internal, nonrational self takes over, and she "runs in panic . . . leaving behind Ronnie's [*sic*] fieldglasses, the symbol of shallow rationality."

16. Crews, *Perils of Humanism,* p. 159, reads the echo as "her unvoiced desire for physical love," and Gransden, *Forster,* p. 97, similarly sees it as "the emptiness of life without sexual desire."

17. Hollingsworth, "The Echoes . . . ," p. 38, notes that "when Aziz shows Fielding the picture of his dead wife, bringing her for the moment from behind the barrier of purdah: '. . . how bewildering she found it, the echoing contradictory

Adela begins to doubt the validity of her accusation at the trial, where the near-naked man who pulls the punkah seems to her to control the proceedings (*P*, p. 217) and to represent physicality, sexuality, and beauty. She seems physical and human for the first time when she resents the anonymous comment that she is uglier than Aziz: "Her body resented being called ugly, and trembled" (*P*, p. 219). A victim of her own repression, she is not purposely persecuting Aziz, as Forster assures us: "Adela had always meant to tell the truth and nothing but the truth" (*P*, p. 227). During the trial, she relives the day in the caves (*P*, p. 227) and immediately admits that she has made a mistake as soon as she realizes that she has, a heroic admission that takes extraordinary courage to make.[18]

After the trial, Adela sits in a carriage next to Fielding, "the heroic Principal" (*P*, p. 233), and she is addressed by some people in the crowd as "Mrs. Moore" (*P*, p. 233). She has achieved something great: she has discovered and acknowledged her own sexuality, and her echo disappears (*P*, p. 239). Fielding for the first time judges that "she had become a real person" (*P*, p. 245). She is now one with Indian women; like them, she gets "the worst of both worlds" (*P*, p. 259). Adela achieves self-knowledge when she realizes that she has a major character defect which would have doomed her marriage and which keeps the Indians from appreciating her sacrifice: she has an undeveloped heart and cannot feel affection or emotion (*P*, pp. 260; 262). In the end, Adela no longer wants love for herself, but she

world' (117). One recalls this phrase when reading later of Adela Quested and her echo; an emancipated English girl, she has entered the world which Aziz' wife only looks out upon, but for her too it is echoing, contradictory, and bewildering."

18. Heilbrun, "The Woman as Hero," pp. 138–39, judges her a hero: "In speaking the truth Adele [*sic*] Quested, the hero of the modern 'quest,' alienates everyone, those who will never forgive her for accusing Aziz, and those who will never forgive her for withdrawing the accusation. As a woman, Adele owes nothing to Aziz. . . . But she will not sacrifice him, even to that fury which hell hath nothing like. She finds her function beyond the range of her womanhood in an act of public heroism."

wants "others to want it" (*P*, p. 263). Incapable of love, she
establishes a friendship with Fielding (*P*, p. 265) that ultimately allows him to love, for Adela introduces him to
Stella, Mrs. Moore's daughter, whom he marries (*P*, p. 302).
Adela herself settles down to a career in England (*P*, p. 262)
and presumably finds whatever happiness there is without
love.

Cyril Fielding is first presented to us, at the Bridge Party,
as a democrat "who talked to anyone" (*P*, p. 45). He, rather
than Adela, is most like the Schlegels, whose commitment to
ideas leads to a belief in sexual and class equality:

> The feeling grew that Mr. Fielding was a disruptive force, and
> rightly, for ideas are fatal to caste, and he used ideas by that most
> potent method—interchange. . . . The remark that did him most
> harm at the club was a silly aside to the effect that the so-called
> white races are really pinko-grey.
>
> [*P*, p. 62]

Like the Schlegels, he is an optimist about personal relations
(*P*, p. 67) and always reacts to individuals, not stereotypes
or roles: he resists both Anglo-India's stereotypes about Indians and Aziz's stereotypes about women. He asserts, "my
job's Education. I believe in teaching people to be individuals, and to understand other individuals. It's the only thing
I do believe in" (*P*, p. 121). At the moment of crisis he
emerges as a hero in Forster's world, for he sticks by his
friend rather than his class and insists on Aziz's innocence
(*P*, p. 163). Like Adela, he resents being labeled: "To slink
through India unlabelled was his aim. Henceforward he
would be called 'anti-British,' 'seditious'—terms that bored
him, and diminished his utility" (*P*, p. 175).

Unlike Aziz, Fielding immediately recognizes Adela's
heroism when she withdraws her charge. He becomes her
only friend in all India, the only person not to see her as a
pariah, for he recognizes her sacrifice: "He had a natural
sympathy for the down-trodden . . . and had determined

not to leave the poor girl in the lurch" (*P,* p. 244). Fielding is the first person to suggest that Adela's charge may have been the result of a hallucination (*P,* p. 239), for he knows both that Aziz did not do what Adela said he did, and that Adela had no malice in her: the truth emerges from personal, not cultural or sexual, analysis. Fielding convinces Aziz to be merciful to Adela (*P,* p. 249), but Aziz assumes an affair between them and infuriates Fielding by calling him a "naughty boy" (*P,* p. 273). To Fielding, as to Margaret Schlegel, "naughtiness" implies a view of life and of sex which must be overcome if personal intercourse, both between the sexes and within the same sex, is to survive (*P,* p. 274).

Fielding's views on posterity throughout the novel reflect those of Margaret Schlegel. Like her, he does not "care for children" (*P,* p. 119) and feels no obligation to do so. He accepts her affirmation of "eternal differences" between people and adds to it an understanding of the nature of imperialism and an avant-garde awareness of the population explosion: "Other people can have children. No obligation, with England getting so chock-a-block and overrunning India for jobs" (*P,* p. 119). Unlike Aziz, who with Gino in *Where Angels Fear to Tread* is obsessed with physical posterity (*P,* p. 119), Fielding believes in spiritual and intellectual heredity: "I'd far rather leave a thought behind me than a child" (*P,* p. 119). In the end he achieves both kinds of posterity, for he and Stella Moore have a son (*P,* p. 307).

Fielding's early prejudice against and cynicism about marriage derive largely from his desire to travel light (*P,* pp. 121; 262). In the course of the novel, however, he discovers that "Travelling light is less easy as soon as affection is involved" (*P,* p. 280). This discovery comes about in relation to his friendship with Aziz, not in relation to a sexual love, but it holds true equally for both. When Fielding marries, we do not react with despair, as we do when Rickie Elliot marries in *The Longest Journey.* Fielding's marriage is a positive step, more like Margaret Schlegel's. It unites him symbolically with Mrs. Moore, with whom previously he has not been really connected, and it in effect brings about his reconciliation with Aziz in the capsizing of boats which leads to baptism and rebirth (*P*, pp. 315–17). By marrying Stella and becoming reconciled with Aziz, Fielding reminds us at the end of what Philip Herriton could have been if he had been able to give up his detachment and embrace both Caroline and Gino. This is not the Philip Herriton that Forster actually portrayed, however, and the ending of *A Passage to India* reflects a corresponding pessimism. In fact, the ending of *A Passage to India* most clearly resembles the actual bleak ending of *Where Angels Fear to Tread* than any other of Forster's novels. The final effect of Fielding's marriage remains unclear to us because it is unclear to him (*P*, p. 318); and the friendship with Aziz, although desired by both, remains finally impossible, as the last words in the novel drive home: "No, not yet . . . No, not there" (*P*, p. 322).

Six
Maurice

The role of homosexuals in *Maurice* parallels women's role in *A Room with a View*. Maurice must be rescued by Alec from conventional antisexuality and from the feeling that homosexuals are somehow evil, just as Lucy must be rescued by George from a comparable antisexuality and from the belief that women are inferior. Maurice Hall must travel down a long, rather convoluted corridor to sexual self-knowledge and, equally important, to the realization that people are and should be allowed to be different. At the end of this hall he joins Margaret Schlegel and Cyril Fielding, the other Forsterian characters to achieve this wisdom. Maurice is not intrinsically as heroic as either Margaret or Fielding, however; his character is more like Lucy Honeychurch's, and he does not come to wisdom easily. Even after he accepts his own difference, he assumes the existence of a conformity within deviance, as earlier he assumed a conformity within conventionality. Before he can realize that difference is acceptable, and even desirable, he must realize that it exists everywhere, a knowledge he does not attain until late in the novel:

Maurice had the Englishman's inability to conceive variety. His troubles had taught him that other people are alive, but not yet that they are different, and he attempted to regard Clive's development as a forerunner of his own.[1]

1. E. M. Forster, *Maurice* (New York, Norton, 1971), p. 161. All future references to this work will appear in the text in the abbreviated form *M*. A Signet paperback edition is also available.

Maurice presents us with three distinct sexual types: (1) Maurice, who is at first bewildered and disoriented, then exclusively homosexual, platonically and then physically; (2) Clive Durham, who is at first exclusively homosexual, but in the idealistic, philosophic sense only, and then is exclusively heterosexual, both philosophically and physically; and (3) Alec Scudder, who is bisexual and consistently physical. The world of *Maurice* has room for all kinds, as Maurice finally realizes. At the end of the novel, in response to Alec's claim that "It is natural to want a girl, you cannot go against human nature" (*M*, p. 216), Maurice finally accepts Margaret Schlegel's philosophy of tolerance and asserts, "I have really got to think that 'natural' only means oneself" (*M*, p. 222).

When the novel opens, Maurice is nearly fifteen years old and is about to graduate from a preparatory school to a public school, from celibacy to sexuality (*M*, pp. 9–10). Mr. Ducie, one of Maurice's teachers, takes it upon himself to aid in this transition by teaching Maurice about sex, but his approach is hypocritical from the beginning:

"When I was your age, my father told me something that proved very useful and helped me a good deal." This was untrue: his father had never told him anything. But he needed a prelude to what he was going to say.

[*M*, p. 13]

Maurice's first exposure is to sex that exists for the express purpose of reproduction. He later despairs when he realizes that *his* sexuality will never people the earth, for Mr. Ducie "spoke of male and female, created by God in the beginning in order that the earth might be peopled" (*M*, p. 13).

Mr. Ducie's sexuality, although heterosexual, is unconnected with women: he tells Maurice, "It is not a thing that your mother can tell you, and you should not mention it to her nor to any lady" (*M*, p. 13). The implications of this statement are twofold: first, sexuality is somehow evil or dirty and men should not mention it in mixed company; and second, ladies should not know about it at all, as indeed Clive's wife later in the novel does not. Mr. Ducie's insistence on a discretion which seems more like secrecy implies that for him the knowledge of sexuality is not integral but is rather a set of unconnected diagrams which have no relation to life. Henry Wilcox's sexual inadequacies become much more understandable if we realize that this is the sort of sexual education he probably received.

The diagrams Mr. Ducie draws in the sand are meaningless to Maurice (*M,* pp. 13–14), and he does not respond with the expected questions (*M,* p. 14); even this early in the novel he is different. Mr. Ducie sees sexuality as "rather a bother" but as a necessary prelude to "the great things—Love, Life" (*M,* p. 14), his unreal vision of which discredits him in our eyes: "He spoke of the ideal man—chaste with asceticism. He sketched the glory of Woman" (*M,* p. 14). Mr. Ducie propounds a chivalry Forster rejects: "To love a noble woman, to protect and serve her—this, he told the little boy, was the crown of life" (*M,* pp. 14–15); later, when Clive rejects Maurice and succumbs to the Duciedom of chivalry (*M,* pp. 129–30), he, too, loses our sympathy. Mr. Ducie's simplistic raptures about heterosexual love mean nothing to Maurice, and their exchange is revealing:

"God's in his heaven, All's right with the world. Male and female! Ah wonderful!"
    "I think I shall not marry," remarked Maurice.
                                                                    [*M,* p. 15]

Mr. Ducie assumes that Maurice's comment reflects merely a child's lack of interest in sex, and he invites Maurice and his wife to dinner "ten years hence" (*M,* p. 15). Maurice "smiled with pleasure" (*M,* p. 15) at the invitation; but the person with whom he will meet Mr. Ducie in ten years' time is Alec Scudder, in the British Museum. In a sense Mr.

Ducie himself assures this outcome, for just as the young Maurice begins to contemplate marriage for the first time, Mr. Ducie's hypocrisy takes over and he panics at the realization that he "never scratched out those infernal diagrams" (*M,* p. 15), and a lady is approaching! Maurice allays his fears by assuring him that "The tide'll have covered them by now" (*M,* p. 15); the tide functions symbolically as the tide of Maurice's homosexuality, which washes out the wonder of male and female before a lady can approach it. Only Maurice, not Mr. Ducie, is aware of the unreality and impermanence of heterosexual diagrams, and he also appreciates the hyoocrisy of his teacher: " 'Liar,' he thought. 'Liar, coward, he's told me nothing' " (*M,* p. 15). Maurice returns to the "darkness" of childlike asexuality (*M,* p. 15), but he has already rejected Mr. Ducie's brand of heterosexuality.

The image of darkness continues throughout the novel and at times seems an allegorical symbol for homosexuality. When Maurice graduates from preparatory school, the other boys "showered presents on him, declaring he was brave. A great mistake—he wasn't brave: he was afraid of the dark. But no one knew this" (*M,* p. 11). His childlike pretense of bravery parallels the pretense of heterosexuality against which Maurice ultimately rebels, as going to bed in the dark parallels the acceptance of homosexuality, an acceptance which at this point is reluctant and contrasted to "manhood":

When Maurice did go to bed, it was reluctantly. . . . He had been such a man all the evening, but the old feeling came over him as soon as his mother had kissed him good night. The trouble was the looking-glass.

[*M,* p. 19]

What Maurice fears is his double, or *homo,* in the mirror. This fear of his reflection is symbolic of the plight of all young homosexuals, as Lilia's reflection on her plight in

Where Angels Fear to Tread reflects the plight of all women. Only when Maurice accepts his homosexuality can he look in the mirror with satisfaction (*M*, p. 115), when he is in love with Clive. The young Maurice can bear total darkness (*M*, p. 19), the darkness of presexuality; but across from his bedroom is a street lamp which forces him to accept the knowledge of his own nature, and which he can later gaze at confidently with Clive's letters in his pocket (*M*, p. 53). When Clive rejects Maurice and leaves "the darkness within for that without," Maurice begins again to doubt himself and feel damned: "It was so late that the lamps had been extinguished in the suburban roads, and total night without compromise weighed on him, as on his friend" (*M*, p. 130).

Maurice loses the light within when he loses Clive (*M*, p. 139), but the image of light and dark changes at this point in the novel. In the light of a self-knowledge which Maurice has internalized and which will not be wished away, darkness itself becomes a positive force: "Ah for darkness— not the darkness of a house . . . but the darkness where he can be free!" (*M*, p. 191). When Alec's boat sails without Alec on it, the sun comes out for the first time since Clive rejected Maurice (*M*, p. 238). Maurice no longer needs artificial light; he *knows* himself finally, and he makes the ultimate connection when he knows without even receiving Alec's wire where to find his lover: asleep in the boathouse, "just visible in the last dying of the day" (*M*, p. 240).

Maurice's ultimate acceptance of his homosexuality and of a lower-class lover is foreshadowed in the figure of George, the garden boy. When the young Maurice's mother announces her intention of giving Maurice "a lovely time," his response is immediately to ask, "Where's George?" (*M*, p. 17). Only by thinking of George, "just a common servant" (*M*, p. 20), can Maurice fall asleep in his dark room. Maurice's final triumphant connection with Alec overcomes his early snobbery, and he finally realizes the impossibility of referring to anyone as "just a common servant," for the acceptance of homosexuality leads to the further discovery of the falsity of class values when compared to human ones. We see this happening quite early in the novel: the young Maurice speaks to servants in a different voice from the one he uses for gentlefolk *except* when he asks about George, and then his voice becomes natural (*M*, p. 18).[2]

The adolescent Maurice has two dreams, both significant and both homosexual:

In the first dream he felt very cross. He was playing football against a nondescript whose existence he resented. He made an effort and the nondescript turned into George, that garden boy. But he had to be careful or it would reappear. George headed down the field towards him, naked and jumping over the wood-stacks. "I shall go mad if he turns wrong now," said Maurice, and just as they collared this happened, and a brutal disappointment woke him up.

[*M*, p. 22]

Maurice both desires and fears physical contact; he resents a generalized homosexuality in the image of a nondescript adversary but accepts it in the image of a focused, personal object, the naked George. His second dream is less explicit: "Nothing happened. He scarcely saw a face, scarcely heard a voice say, 'That is your friend,' and then it was over, having filled him with beauty and taught him tenderness" (*M*, p. 22).

"The Friend" is a Persian expression for God (*P*, p. 277), and in *A Passage to India* the desire for a friend runs parallel to the desire for a sexual partner, in Aziz's case a woman. After Aziz writes a poem expressing his "need for the

2. Frank Kermode, "A Queer Business," *Atlantic Monthly*, Nov. 1, 1971, p. 141, points out that "the book concerns itself with the relation between homosexual Freedom and the breaking down of class barriers. In the end Maurice acknowledges his love for a successor to George and goes off to live with him." Noel Annan, "Love Story," *New York Review of Books*, Oct. 21, 1971, p. 17, correctly asserts that "Forster's novels are about many things but always about class. It is as essential to him that Maurice's lover should be working-class as it is that he be a man."

Friend who never comes yet is not entirely disproved" (*P*, p. 106), he thinks of women in a different way, "less definite, more intense" (*P*, p. 106). The desire for "the Ideal Friend" is a commonplace of idealized homosexuality also; [3] as Mrs. Moore realizes, all love is the same.[4]

During his public school years, Maurice seems in almost every way an average adolescent, and his popularity rests on his ordinariness (*M*, p. 25). He has not yet developed any sympathy for the underdog and is a bit of a bully (*M*, p. 21), like Gerald Dawes in *The Longest Journey*. Forster stresses that in Maurice's case brutality "was against his nature. But it was necessary at school, or he might have gone under" (*M*, p. 30). Forster's indictment is more of the public school system than of Maurice, and indeed Maurice stops being a bully as soon as he arrives at Cambridge (*M*, p. 30). In fact, Maurice emerges from the ordeal rather well, when contrasted with Clive, who never does develop any sympathy for the oppressed. Maurice's sexual bewilderment (*M*, p. 21) and obscenity (*M*, p. 23) at public school are not signs of inherent homosexuality but rather of general adolescence; even the fact that his crushes are on other boys (*M*, p. 24) is not definitive at this stage, but rather a natural outgrowth of the segregation of the sexes: there are no girls around to have crushes on.[5]

When Maurice graduates from public school, his normal homosexual dreams and crushes are thrust up against society's heterosexual expectations. When Dr. Barry implies an affair between Maurice and the housemaster's wife,

3. J. R. Ackerley, *My Father and Myself* (New York, Coward-McCann, 1969), p. 124.
4. George Steiner, "Under the Greenwood Tree," *New Yorker*, Oct. 9, 1971, p. 166, reads *A Passage to India* in light of *Maurice*: "The non-event in the hills of Marabar comprises values that we can now confidently recognize as being both heterosexual and homosexual. Both are facets, momentary and—it may be—contingent, of the unbounded unity of love." Kermode, "A Queer Business," p. 142, further points out that "the coming of the friend, recurrent in Maurice, is a theme Forster realized finally in the coming of Krishna, after many failed invocations, in *A Passage to India*."
5. Annan, "Love Story," p. 13.

Maurice thinks of heterosexual sex apparently for the first time. His reaction is "a violent repulsion . . . he had remembered Mr. Ducie's diagrams" (*M,* p. 28). Dr. Barry, like everyone else, expects Maurice to be like his father, and Maurice for the first time realizes the unlikelihood of his ever being so. He knows at this point that he cannot fulfill society's role expectations, and Dr. Barry, who "went on lecturing him," "said much that gave pain" (*M,* p. 28).

Maurice inherits his ordinariness from his father, and presumably would develop into another dreary Mr. Hall senior if he were not "different." Maurice's father traverses the ordinary route from homosexual to heterosexual love, but Maurice does not make that transition and thus is saved: "Mr. Hall senior had neither fought nor thought; there had never been any occasion; he has supported society and moved without a crisis from illicit to licit love" (*M,* p. 151). In *Maurice,* as in *A Room with a View,* the flesh educates the spirit, and Maurice's father's ghost envies his son's salvation from the fate of an undeveloped heart:

Now, looking across at his son, he is touched with envy, the only pain that survives in the world of shades. For he sees the flesh educating the spirit, as his has never been educated, and developing the sluggish heart and the slack mind against their will.

[*M,* pp. 151–52]

Maurice's salvation develops in two stages, with two mentors: Clive teaches him to accept his homosexuality; Alec, his sexuality.

Maurice's rejection of conventional religion is closely bound up with his homosexuality: "Maurice's father was becoming a pillar of Church and Society when he died, and other things being alike Maurice would have stiffened too" (*M,* p. 46). But other things are not alike, and Maurice damns the church for damning him near the end of the novel, when "the church," not the church *bell,* forces Alec to leave Maurice's bed (*M,* p. 196).

Agnosticism and homosexuality are also closely linked in Clive, who states explicitly that his rejection of religion is due to his homosexuality, or rather to religion's view of his homosexuality (*M*, p. 70). The Holy Communion which first Clive and then Maurice refuse to take suggests communion with women, holy in Duciedom. Only Maurice, however, has the courage to carry his rebellion to its logical conclusion and refuse also to go through the (for them) hypocritical forms of a heterosexual life. The primary difference between Clive and Maurice emerges when we see with what they replace the Christianity they reject: Clive a philosophical Hellenism; Maurice a personal love for an individual. Clive's Hellenism is as antisexual as conventional Christianity, and the most passionate scene he has with Maurice is consummated by a discussion of the Trinity:

"You wanted to get it and you're going to," said Durham, sporting the door.
Maurice went cold and then crimson. But Durham's voice, when he next heard it, was attacking his opinions on the Trinity.
[*M*, p. 47]

In *Maurice*, as elsewhere, Forster sees the rejection of Christianity as a step toward salvation, but although both Clive and Maurice reject Christianity, only Maurice is saved.

Clive gains the courage to reject Christianity through the example of Risley (*M*, p. 71), an important catalyst in *Maurice*. Maurice's acceptance of Risley is Maurice's first rebellious act, and his first unexpected one (*M*, p. 31). He feels that Risley "might help him" (*M*, p. 34), and indeed it is Risley's room that Maurice meets Clive. Later in the novel, when Maurice is terribly lonely, he meets Risley at a performance of Tchaikovsky's Pathetic Symphony (*M*, p. 162), the same symphony Clive was looking for in Risley's room when Maurice met him (*M*, p. 35). At the concert Risley gives Maurice real aid when he tells him enough about Tchaikovsky's life for Maurice to realize the mistake he would be making if he were to attempt heterosexuality without feeling it. Maurice, however, does not like Risley (*M*, p. 162); Forster stresses the crucial point that all homosexuals are not alike and do not necessarily like each other, any more than do all women, all men, or all Indians.

Maurice's heart awakens when he meets Clive: "his heart had lit never to be quenched again, and one thing in him at last was real" (*M*, p. 40); Maurice does not have the heart disease of Sawston, Charles Wilcox, and Anglo-India. Although Cambridge provides the atmosphere in which Maurice can discover that people are real (*M*, p. 30), Clive, who represents Cambridge (*M*, p. 251), can never do the same himself. Like Rickie Elliot, he sees people merely as images.

Before Clive's articulation of love, the imagery of their relationship is of the hunt, or as Forster calls it, "the language of battle" (*M*, p. 41); curiously, it is Maurice who stalks Clive. His hunt is not conscious, however, and he is shocked when Clive puts his feelings into words (*M*, p. 58). Maurice is a nonverbal person who articulates nothing (*M*, p. 41), and he needs Clive to force him to acknowledge consciously what he already knows subconsciously. Their early physical intimacy is not regarded as sexual (*M*, p. 45) and is apparently considered normal, for it "attracted no notice" (*M*, p. 45).

Clive's first mention of homosexuality to Maurice is academic. He resents the fact that Dean Cornwallis, whom Risley has correctly called a "eunuch" (*M*, p. 33), tells his translation class to "Omit: a reference to the unspeakable vice of the Greeks" (*M*, p. 51). Clive insists on his own academic approach: "I regard it as a point of pure scholarship. The Greeks, or most of them, were that way inclined, and to omit it is to omit the mainstay of Athenian society" (*M*, p. 51). This fact is new to Maurice and liberating as a piece of information, but he must wait an awfully long time to find someone whose approach to sex is not academic, as both Mr. Ducie's and Clive's are. Even Clive's protestation of love is academic and has more to do with Plato and *The Symposium* than with Maurice (*M*, p. 58): "books meant so much for him he forgot that they were a bewilderment to others. Had he trusted the body there would have been no disaster" (*M*, p. 73). Clive's approach to love reminds us of Rickie Elliot's; and the description of Cecil Vyse in *A Room with a View* is also applicable: "He is the sort who are all right as long as they keep to things—books, pictures—but kill when they come to people" (*R*, p. 194).[6]

Immediately before Clive tells Maurice of his love, Maurice endures the "Episode of Gladys Olcott" (*M*, p. 53), his first and virtually last foray into the field of heterosexual relationships. He is influenced less by an interest in Miss Olcott than by society's pressure to be interested in her, and since she senses this, "Something went wrong at once" (*M*, p. 54). He plays the role of the domineering male (*M*, p. 54), a societally approved role for which he is not suited, as indeed no one should be. He makes romantic advances as if according to a script (*M*, p. 54), as did Cecil Vyse, and Miss Olcott responds accordingly:

It was not that Miss Olcott objected to having her hand pressed. Others had done it and Maurice could have done it had he guessed how. But she knew something was wrong. His touch revolted her. It was a corpse's.

[*M*, p. 54]

She recognizes something about him that he cannot yet see himself,[7] and he reacts by falling back on "public-schoolishness" (*M*, p. 56):

He was less alert, he again behaved as he supposed he was supposed to behave—a perilous feat for one who is not dowered with

6. Cynthia Ozick, "Forster as Homosexual," *Commentary*, 52 (Dec. 1971), 84.
7. Mrs. Orr refuses Herbert Pembroke's offer of marriage in *The Longest Journey* with a similar vehemence (*LJ*, p. 163); she recognizes Herbert's undeveloped heart as Gladys Olcott recognizes Maurice's homosexuality.

imagination. . . . though Miss Olcott had passed, the insincerity
that led him to her remained.

[*M*, p. 56]

   Maurice exhibits the worst aspects of the Wilcox men
when he dismisses the Howells, long faithful employees,
and "sets up a motorcar instead of a carriage" (*M*, p. 55).
He decides to join his father's stock brokerage firm, "step-
ping into the niche that England had prepared for him"
(*M*, p. 55). Except for his homosexuality, he would fit that
niche perfectly, for he thinks that the car and the firm are
signs of manhood. His real maturation comes later, however, when he attains self-knowledge at Cambridge.
   When Maurice rejects Clive's offer of love, he rejects
spring (*M*, p. 59), the very rejection Mr. Emerson has
warned against in *A Room with a View*. Maurice lives through
a crisis one aspect of which is to feel horror at the idea of
"A man crying!" (*M*, p. 61). Society does not allow men to
show emotion, but Maurice achieves a vision (*M*, p. 62)
which places him outside society's dogmas, and he vows to
end his past hypocrisy:

He would not—and this was the test—pretend to care about
women when the only sex that attracted him was his own. He
loved men and always had loved them. He longed to embrace
them and mingle his being with theirs. . . .
   After this crisis Maurice became a man.

[*M*, pp. 62–63]

He is finally connected, even more connected than Clive
turns out to be, for Clive rejects the physical; Maurice
unites the spiritual and the physical, "idealism and brutality," into love (*M*, p. 63). A man now, he rejects Mr. Ducie:
"There was still much to learn. . . . But he discovered the
method and looked no more at scratches in the sand"
(*M*, p. 63).
   Maurice regains "spring" when he springs through Clive's

window just in time to hear Clive calling his name in a dream (*M,* p. 66). For the first time they call each other by their first names; love triumphs, at least temporarily, but the technical device through which it triumphs is so silly as to practically negate the thematic force. The melodrama of people jumping in and out of windows in *Maurice* fortunately has no parallel in Forster's other novels.[8] We cannot excuse such lapses with the explanation that an unconventional subject requires a conventional technique, which is the only possible explanation; it is more honest to attribute the fact that Maurice "caught hold of the mullion and sprang" (*M,* p. 66) to the book's "considerable loss of the careful distancing that has elsewhere lent Forster's fiction its magnificent clarity and majestic disinterest."[9]

Clive's development is very different from Maurice's. Unlike Maurice, he "suffered little from bewilderment as a boy" (*M,* p. 69), but also unlike Maurice, he never felt anything at all directly. Clive's homosexuality, like the rest of his life, is intellectual, metaphorical, and literary: at first damned by Sodom, he is saved by Plato (*M,* p. 69). Plato liberates him by teaching him the value of differences: " 'To make the most of what I have.' Not to crush it down, not vainly to wish that it was something else, but to cultivate it in such ways as will not vex either God or Man" (*M,* p. 70). Unfortunately, Clive forgets this lesson as soon as he himself is no longer "different"; his intellectuality is purely selfish.

His reaction to Maurice's rejection is genuine (*M,* p. 73), however, and we must sympathize with him. Clive's pain and self-loathing, which will be mirrored in Maurice when Clive rejects him, is a much stronger reaction to rejection than any we see in Forster's heterosexual love affairs. Maurice's rejection of Clive, and the later reversal, both

8. I exempt Forster's sudden deaths from the charge of melodrama, for they emphasize theme rather than undercut it, as here.
9. Joseph Epstein, *"Maurice," New York Times Book Review,* Oct. 10, 1971, p. 28.

express something beyond the rejection of an individual; they both involve the rejection of a style of life, the passing of a moral judgment, and Maurice's "Oh, rot!" (*M*, p. 58) creates in Clive a reborn "sense of sin" (*M*, p. 73).

After Maurice jumps in the window, Clive awakens and "Warmth was upon him" (*M*, p. 74); and warmth is precisely what Maurice gives Clive. Clive is surely more intelligent, but Maurice is warmer, ultimately too warm for the sexually frigid Clive. Their motorcycle ride represents and predicts the course of their relationship. Although Maurice drives, Clive sets the direction (*M*, p. 75), just as he sets the antisexual tone of the relationship (*M*, pp. 93, 98, 151). On the day of their platonic idyll in the country, the motorcycle breaks down, and "A noise arose as of a thousand pebbles being shaken together between [Maurice's] legs" (*M*, p. 76). The motorcycle is Maurice's grandfather's present "against his coming of age" (*M*, p. 77), but it breaks before Maurice's birthday, as Maurice's relationship with Clive breaks before *it* is consummated; the death throes of the motorcycle, signaling sexual death, correspond to Maurice's sexual awakening when Clive rejects him.

Clive explicitly sees the motorcycle as symbol: "Bound in a single motion, they seemed there closer to one another than elsewhere; the machine took on a life of its own, in which they met and realized the unity preached by Plato" (*M*, p. 80). This view reveals the central flaw in Clive and in any relationship with him, for he desires union in an asexual machine rather than in physical, sexual love. When one considers Forster's views on motorcars in *Howards End,* the condemnation of Clive is complete. The car is a negative entity, not a proper means of connecting two people. When Maurice's motorcycle breaks down, it becomes parallel to the car from which Margaret Schlegel jumps, which was taking her to Henry Wilcox. Margaret, more heroic than Maurice, manages eventually to overcome Henry's antisexuality, but Maurice cannot change Clive and must reach his own sexual connection with someone else.

Maurice's mechanical relationship with Clive contrasts well with his later, more natural one with Alec, where two lovers, physical lovers, live together in the greenwood. Clive's attempt to use a motorcycle to effect the unity taught by premechanical Plato is rather absurd. He correctly sees that he needs something beyond books to effect platonic love and unity in the modern world, that Plato is not sufficient by itself. But Clive makes the wrong choice. What is needed to realize platonic unity is not mechanization, which is surely lacking in Plato, but physical love, which is somewhat lacking in Plato and even more so in Clive.

One positive result of Maurice's outing with Clive is the confrontation with Dr. Barry, in which Maurice rejects chivalry. Maurice is sent down from Cambridge for his rudeness to Dean Cornwallis (*M,* p. 79), a "eunuch" who resents even platonic homosexual love affairs (*M,* pp. 79–80), and Maurice's mother delegates the job of chastising her son to Dr. Barry, a neighbor and surrogate father. Dr. Barry tells Maurice that he is "a disgrace to chivalry" (*M,* p. 85) for hurting his mother by not apologizing to the Dean, and this accusation begins a new and critical chain of thought in Maurice's mind:

"A disgrace to chivalry." He considered the accusation. If a woman had been in that side-car, if then he had refused to stop at the Dean's bidding, would Dr. Barry have required an apology from him? Surely not. He followed out this train of thought with difficulty. His brain was still feeble. But he was obliged to use it, for so much in current speech and ideas needed translation before he could understand them.

[*M,* p. 85]

Maurice's "difference" forces him to develop his intelligence and to question society's arbitrary judgments. When he re-

turns from Dr. Barry's, his mother senses that he "had
grown up," and his sisters "had a sense of some change in
his mouth and eyes and voice since he had faced Dr. Barry"
(*M*, p. 85).

Mrs. Hall is more concerned about the loss of Maurice's
motorcycle than she is about the loss of his degree when he
is sent down from Cambridge (*M*, p. 82). Like Mrs. Herriton and Lilia in *Where Angels Fear to Tread,* Mrs. Hall's life
centers around her home: "Church was the only place Mrs.
Hall had to go to—the shops delivered" (*M*, p. 16). If Mr.
Hall, senior, has no demands on him to develop any individuality or real humanity, Mrs. Hall has even fewer. In the
world of *Maurice,* women barely exist, for they live two
stages removed from the novel's main concern, the problems of male homosexuals.

Forster briefly touches on women's problems when he
discusses Kitty's financial dependence on her brother. Even
her hardly radical desire to go to an institute to study "Domestic Economy" (*M*, p. 122) is dependent on his whim, and
he thwarts her for no real reason. Only after he is rejected
by Clive can he sympathize with another person's frustration and grant Kitty the right to live the life she wants
(*M*, p. 142). Kitty is the more intelligent of Maurice's two
sisters, but Ada's beauty makes her their grandfather's
heiress.

Maurice sees Ada as the ultimate sexual stereotype, Eve
the temptress, and unfairly blames her for breaking up his
"friendship" with Clive (*M*, p. 134). Clive also uses Ada unfairly, and she is hurt by his withdrawal (*M*, p. 142). Clive,
who cannot see men as real, has even more trouble with
women; he does not consider Ada a person but merely a
transition (*M*, p. 130). He never gets in touch with her even
to tell her that "circumstances" do not allow their relationship to continue, but cruelly says nothing at all and lets
her wonder, for she does not really exist to him. Like Indian women in *A Passage to India,* women in *Maurice* are

oppressed both by society in general and by the oppressed men in that society.

Clive, like Ansell, is an outright misogynist, but Maurice is less so (*M,* p. 100). Clive can never tolerate differences: when he is homosexual, all women are awful; when he is heterosexual, all homosexuals are awful. The homosexual Clive assumes that women cannot understand the "harmony" of homosexual love, a harmony which in his hands turns into precisely the "starved medievalism" he says it is not (*M,* p. 90). He takes out his antagonism toward his mother and sister on all women. Maurice is more open and heroic; he condemns some women, but not all (*M,* p. 52). Maurice, unlike Clive, can react individually. Clive's attitude toward Kitty when he becomes a heterosexual is telling: "He had always cared for Kitty least of the family—she was not a true woman, as he called it now" (*M,* p. 121). No definition of "true woman" is forthcoming. Presumably, Kitty is simply too intelligent to fit Clive's stereotyped demands.

Women function negatively in *Maurice* as the constant reminder of society's heterosexual expectations; Clive's mother spends the first half of the novel pressuring Clive to marry. Mrs. Durham, as a widow, has no defined position in society and must live, emotionally and financially, through her children: "Oh, Penge is his absolutely, under my husband's will. I must move to the dower house as soon as he marries" (*M,* p. 95). Like Mrs. Herriton, she exists by manipulating others: "Mrs. Durham did not propose to retire to the dower house in practice, whatever she might do in theory, and believed she could best manage Clive through his wife" (*M,* p. 101). When Clive does marry, Mrs. Durham remains at Penge but loses her power: "though Clive's mother no longer presided she remained in residence, owing to the dower house drains" (*M,* p. 166).

The Durhams' class of society is losing control of an England that is being run more and more by Wilcoxes, but Mrs. Durham retains her snobbery toward the lower classes.

She is rude to her servants, speaking French in front of Alec (*M*, p. 172), as Herbert Pembroke does before Rickie's bedder in *The Longest Journey*. Herself a victim of society's oppression of women, Mrs. Durham, like the British women in *A Passage to India*, epitomizes society's oppression of the lower classes. She cannot understand why Alec wants to emigrate and live for himself (*M*, p. 189) any more than the early Maurice could understand why Kitty wanted to go to school and learn to do something.

Mrs. Durham's desire for an heir to Penge leads to Maurice's first awareness of the physical sterility that is a necessary corollary to exclusive homosexuality (*M*, pp. 96–97). His reaction is "immense sadness" and a feeling of inadequacy: "His mother or Mrs. Durham might lack mind or heart, but they had done visible work; they had handed on the torch their sons would tread out" (*M*, p. 97). This recognition parallels Rickie Elliot's:

Abram and Sarai were sorrowful, yet their seed became as sand of the sea, and distracts the politics of Europe at this moment. But a few verses of poetry is all that survives of David and Jonathan.

[*LJ*, p. 69]

The novel *Maurice* is Forster's "few verses of poetry."

Ironically, Maurice spends his first day with Alec hunting physical fertility in the shape of rabbits, a hunt prudently arranged by Clive (*M*, p. 173). Whether Maurice is trying to catch fertility or kill it is unclear, but the former is more likely, for Maurice at this point is going to a hypnotist to try to become "normal." While Maurice is hunting rabbits, Alec seems to be hunting Maurice, and their later discussion of fertility in the British Museum furthers their comradeship, friendship, and childless homosexual love (*M*, p. 222).

Forster clearly does not like enforced physical sterility and presents it as a real problem, but his final judgment considers other things more important: variety, difference, and love, both heterosexual and homosexual. Forster did not think homosexuality "wrong: naturally wrong, with the sort of naturalness he did not expect to date," [10] but rather agreed with Stewart Ansell in *The Longest Journey* that "The point is, not what's ordained by nature or any other fool, but what's right" (*LJ*, p. 87); and right for Forster means right for each individual. Sterility may be a greater problem for Maurice than it is for Margaret Schlegel, and it may be the most difficult part of his homosexuality to accept, but his ultimate acceptance of difference does lead to an acceptance even of sterility (*M*, p. 222).[11]

Clive's change to heterosexuality is sudden and linked to the image of religious communion. At the height of their homosexual love, Clive serves Maurice coffee in their suite at Penge (*M*, p. 91); and "coffee" "comes from the Arabic word for wine." [12] Clive offers only the blood, not the body, and prevents the communion from ever being complete. When Clive accepts Mr. Ducie's idea of holy communion, he rejects Maurice's:

The heat at dinner! The voices of the Halls! Their laughter! Maurice's anecdote! It mixed with the food—was the food. Unable to distinguish matter from spirit, he fainted.

[*M*, p. 119]

In religious communion, too, matter equals spirit; but Clive can never accept homosexual matter and becomes hysterical

10. Ozick, "Forster as Homosexual," p. 84.
11. For a further discussion of whether homosexuality is natural or unnatural, see Edward Carpenter, *Homogenic Love, and Its Place in a Free Society* (Manchester, England, The Labour Press Society Limited, 1894), pp. 25–43. Forster's ideas on the subject are much closer to Carpenter's than to Ozick's, and Forster himself attributes the inspiration for the novel *Maurice* to a visit to Carpenter's home (*M*, pp. 249–50). Interestingly, Carpenter, pp. 42–43, contends that "just as the ordinary sex-love has a special function in the propagation of the race, so the other love should have its special function . . . in the generation—not of bodily children—but of those children of the mind, the philosophical conceptions and ideals which transform our lives and those of society."
12. William York Tindall, *A Reader's Guide to James Joyce* (New York, Noonday-Farrar, Straus and Giroux, 1959), p. 216.

when Maurice kisses him (*M*, p. 108). Maurice Christopher, Christ-bearer, carries Clive to bed.

After his faint, Clive gains "the knowledge that love had died" (*M*, p. 119), and his reaction is to become cruel (*M*, p. 111). Reminding us of Philip Herriton in *Where Angels Fear to Tread,* Clive reveals more about himself than he knows when he expresses his wistful longing for an un-lived life:

Happiness! A casual tickling of someone or something against oneself—that's all. Would that we had never been lovers! For then, Maurice, you and I should have lain still and been quiet. We should have slept.

[*M*, p. 113]

We learn at the end of their affair that Clive and Maurice sleep in separate rooms on the Wednesdays they spend at Clive's flat (*M*, p. 115). The night before Clive leaves for Greece, he comes into Maurice's bed, presumably for the first time; and a most peculiar scene ensues:

"I'm cold and miserable generally. I can't sleep. I don't know why."
Maurice did not misunderstand him. He knew and shared his opinions on this point. They lay side by side without touching. Presently Clive said, "It's no better here. I shall go." Maurice was not sorry, for he could not get to sleep either, though for a dif-ferent reason, and he was afraid Clive might hear the drumming of his heart, and guess what it was.

[*M*, p. 115]

Apparently Clive feels a sexual urge and realizes that he must either copulate with Maurice or become heterosexual and copulate with a woman. When he gets into bed with Maurice, he cannot go through with the physical homosex-ual act, so he goes to Greece and sends Maurice a letter say-ing he has become "normal" (*M*, p. 116).

Maurice's reaction to his scene in bed with Clive is as

peculiar as Clive's. He apparently wants to have sexual intercourse but doesn't think he ought to because of Clive's teaching; yet the implication remains that he would if Clive would. Clive, on the other hand, also doesn't think he ought to and really will not.

Forster's terminology for Clive's change is ambiguous: "Clive did not give in to the life spirit without a struggle. He believed in the intellect and tried to think himself back into the old state" (*M*, p. 120). Clive's central problem, like Adela Quested's in *A Passage to India,* is his reliance on the intellect at the expense of the emotions. The "life spirit" is not necessarily heterosexuality, as it seems at first; it refers instead to sexuality, regardless of focus. Clive exists in a world of bizarre morality. He attempts to fight his change to "normality," and his time in bed with Maurice is a battle in that fight, but it reveals the sickness of the mind formulating the strategy: "he could not recall it without disgust. Not until all emotion had ebbed would it have been possible. He regretted it deeply" (*M*, p. 120). Apparently Clive can consider sex only when there is no love, a level of morality significantly less connected than Maurice's. Maurice wants to copulate with Clive when he loves him and is only ashamed of his sexual urges when they are directed at someone he does not love, like Dickie. He is disgusted at Dr. Barry's acceptance of prostitution (*M*, p. 160), and prostitution is essentially what Clive's attitude toward homosexual sex turns out to be.

Clive does not realize that what he is attempting to preserve is an incomplete relationship. He is humiliated by his change precisely because he is not internally connected: "It humiliated him, for he had understood his soul, or, as he said, himself, ever since he was fifteen" (*M*, p. 118). But "the body is deeper than the soul" (*M*, p. 118), and Clive is a slave to his body, if not while he is homosexual, at least in his leaving of that state. The change takes him by surprise because he has ignored his body all along. The body demands fulfillment, as Mr. Emerson stressed in *A Room with a View*, but Clive cannot accept homosexual physical fulfillment.

Clive first notices his change when he is ill, a significant comment by Forster on the natural-unnatural aspect of the homosexuality controversy. His change comes about through his attraction to his nurse, a woman playing what he sees as the ultimate woman's role, that of mother: "He noticed how charming his nurse was and enjoyed obeying her" (*M*, p. 118). Clive prefers the easier mother-child relationship to the more difficult comradeship he attempts with Maurice; and immediately before his confrontation with his former lover, he "submitted his body to be bound" with bandages by Maurice's mother and sisters (*M*, p. 123).

Clive finds heterosexuality easier in another sense also, for women understand and respond to his advances as men never had (*M*, p. 118); he realizes that heterosexuality gives him many more opportunities to make contacts. However, this heterosexuality is exclusive, in a pejorative sense, and dulls his critical judgments; after his change, he goes to a movie which is bad artistically, but he feels a kinship with the moviemaker and the other viewers: "they knew, and he was one of them" (*M*, p. 119). The phrase "one of them" reminds us of Forster's description of Ronny as "one of us" in *A Passage to India* (*P*, p. 25), and suggests a further ironic parallel to *Lord Jim*.[13] Clive uses this feeling of belonging to justify his cruelty to Maurice as Ronny uses his to justify his cruelty to Indians, but in Forster's world cruelty is never justifiable.

Clive's change of sexual focus marks his transition from idealist to hypocrite, with no stop at individualist: "Greece had been clear but dead. He liked the atmosphere of the North, whose gospel is not truth, but compromise" (*M*, p. 121).[14] From this point "Henceforward Clive deteriorates"

13. Howarth, Nov. 22, 1967.
14. Annan, "Love Story," p. 15, points out that in Greece, "bogus literary ideas have come between him and reality," and he sees only death.

(*M*, p. 251), echoing Forster's judgment of Rickie Elliot: "Henceforward he deteriorates. . . . the spiritual part of him proceeded towards ruin" (*LJ*, pp. 209–10). Clive's deterioration is due to his inability to see that the spiritual part of him is not all, that it is precisely *part* of him. After his return from Greece, he is glad to be cut off from Maurice on the telephone, glad to have a bad connection, for as with Rickie, "the approach of reality alarmed him" (*M*, p. 124). Clive and Rickie have much in common: they are both classicists; they both care for images of people rather than for people themselves; and they both make an incorrect choice, give up a male friend for a wife, and then deteriorate. The primary difference between them comes at the ends of the novels: Rickie is somehow redeemed, Clive not at all.

Clive does not escape from Maurice's reality without a scene. The Maurice who tries to convince Clive to continue their love appears "like an immense animal in his fur coat" (*M*, p. 126); and although he sheds his coat, his animal exterior, Clive remains adamant and impersonal. Indeed, his letter of rejection from Greece is impersonal (*M*, p. 116), and Clive continues that tone in their confrontation (*M*, p. 126). Maurice will not physically accept the impersonal, and although his tone "too was impersonal," he keeps touching: "he had not got off the chair" (*M*, p. 127). The previously inarticulate Maurice now believes in the power of personal intercourse, and his comment to Clive is moving: "One ought to talk, talk, talk—provided one has someone to talk to, as you and I have. If you'd have told me, you would have been right by now" [15] (*M*, p. 127). That Clive does not tell Maurice about his feeling until the change is irrevocable sheds an interesting light on their relationship: Clive never thinks of Maurice as a person to "talk to" but rather an image to talk at.

Clive's cruelty and condescension at this point are striking. He totally dissociates himself from his lover; when

15. It is significant that Maurice assumes "right" can be homosexual.

Maurice makes the parallel between Clive's change and his own brief fling with Miss Olcott, Clive cuts him short and calls him childish: "I know my own mind. . . . I was never like you" (*M*, p. 128). Clive obviously never really loves Maurice, but merely worships an image of a Greek god. He is self-centered and cruel: Maurice's interest in a woman is obviously a stupid mistake; Clive's, the will of "the power that governs Man" (*M*, p. 127).

Although Clive tries to remain impersonal in a very personal situation, he is not above using the personal to wound. He cruelly mentions his attraction to Ada (*M*, p. 128) and then attempts to revert immediately to the impersonal, but the impersonal to which he reverts is sheer hypocrisy: he tells Maurice that he likes him "enormously" when he does not like him at all; and he tells Maurice that "character, not passion" is "the real bond" (*M*, p. 128) when he has just shown his total lack of character. His speech continues: "You can't build a house on the sand, and passion's sand. We want bed rock" (*M*, p. 129). His reference to sand reminds us of Mr. Ducie, for a house on the sand is precisely what Clive chooses here; his version of "bed rock" attempts to ignore bed love.

At the end of their scene, Maurice attempts to summon Ada, and Clive becomes completely despicable, for "chivalry had awoken at last. 'You can't drag in a woman,' he breathed; 'I won't have it' " (*M*, p. 129). Clive, who can never react to individuals as individuals, falls back at this time of stress on the ultimate archaism of role-playing, on a chivalry which Maurice rejected a long time ago. Clive has learned nothing from being different. He now gives in completely to society's roles and leaves the Halls, "Asserting a man's prerogative" (*M*, p. 130). Even less connected than before, he still thinks of images, not people, and goes off to look for "some goddess of the new universe" (*M*, p. 130) to replace Maurice. Maurice's last words to Clive here, "Arrange . . . I'm done for" (Forster's ellipses; *M*, p. 130), function as irony, for in the terms of the novel's morality, Clive, not Maurice, is done for.

After Clive's change, he can no longer "penetrate into Maurice's mind" (*M*, p. 136), but we are not convinced that he ever could. He sees Maurice, like Ada, as a transition and not a person: "But for Maurice he would never have developed into being worthy of Anne. His friend had helped him through three barren years" (*M*, p. 163). But those years are essentially "barren" because of Clive's platonic asexuality. Clive does not even give Maurice the courtesy of a personal letter to announce his engagement (*M*, p. 146); like Ada, Maurice is a nonperson. When Clive does telephone, Maurice is eighth on his list (*M*, p. 152). Although Clive is every bit as much a transition for Maurice— from confused, amorphous asexuality to focused, physical homosexuality with Alec—Maurice never sees him in those terms, but always as a person.

Clive's marriage is gruesome in the extreme. His wife is introduced to us erroneously as "Lady Anne Woods" (*M*, p. 145), and she indeed proves to be more of a lady than a woman. In a rather peculiar irony, both Maurice and Clive end up in some sense in the woods, but there the parallel ceases. At the beginning of Clive's relationship with Anne, Clive's position as a homosexual is similar to Lucy's as a woman in *A Room with a View:* there, although Cecil admits a former affair, Lucy is expected to be untouched; here, Anne admits a former "peccadillo," but Clive's homosexual affair with Maurice is unmentionable (*M*, p. 164). Clive himself distorts the past and sees his affair with Maurice as "sentimental" and therefore deserving of "oblivion" (*M*, p. 164). In reality, no relationship could possibly be more "sentimental" than Clive's with Anne; and whatever "sentimentality" (in a negative sense) there was in his relationship with Maurice was the result of Clive's refusal to let the relationship develop beyond the sentimental into the physical.

Anne's own sexuality is pathetic: "When he arrived in her room after marriage, she did not know what he wanted. Despite an elaborate education, no one had told her about sex" (*M*, p. 164). Her lack of sexual education parallels Maurice's inability to find any information about homosexuality. In the world of *Maurice,* sex is to women what homosexuality is to men, considered by society dirty and depraved.

When Anne and Clive do establish a sexual relationship, it is furtive and unconnected, like Henry Wilcox's in *Howards End.* There it is the man who is unconnected, here primarily the woman, but Clive does not try to help Anne connect, as Margaret does Henry. "They united in a world that bore no reference to the daily, and this secrecy drew after it much else of their lives. So much could never be mentioned. He never saw her naked, nor she him" (*M*, p. 164). This last is a great lack when one considers Forster's belief in the power of naked human beauty, which we see in *A Room with a View* and *A Passage to India.* That Anne and Clive "ignored the reproductive and the digestive functions" (*M*, p. 164) unites them with Miss Alan in *A Room with a View,* who is shocked at Mr. Emerson's use of the word "stomach."

Clive's antisexuality is inescapable when he accepts Anne's lack of connection: "though he valued the body the actual deed of sex seemed to him unimaginative, and best veiled in night" (*M*, p. 165). His view of sex emerges as basically Pauline rather than platonic: "Between men it is inexcusable, between man and woman it may be practised since nature and society approve, but never discussed nor vaunted" (*M*, p. 165). His early platonic homosexuality is merely an unsuccessful attempt to escape sexuality altogether. Clive is literal as well as literary: the Greeks do not mention the possibility of a spiritual love between man and woman, so it does not occur to him. In *The Symposium,* sexual love between men and sexual love between man and woman are equal to each other, and both are less than spiritual love between men. Clive's interpretation, however, is Christian and not Greek. Although he does not accept the idea of spiritual love between man and woman or sexual love between man and man, he considers sexual love between man and woman acceptable (barely) and higher than spiritual love between men. Clive's homosexuality is merely a stage he passes through, an aspect of an inaccurate and incomplete Hellenism. When Clive considers his love for Anne exalted rather than debased, he reveals himself as having been a conventional chivalrous Christian all along, and thus reaches a state of conventional stasis: "Beautiful conventions received them—while beyond the barrier Maurice wandered, the wrong words on his lips and the wrong desires in his heart, and his arms full of air" (*M*, p. 165).

Maurice is better off without Clive and develops beyond him, for their platonic affair expresses Clive, not him (*M*, p. 151). Maurice, who is happy in a platonic love relationship, assumes that platonism is necessary for happiness, but in fact he is happy with Clive *in spite of* the platonic nature of their affair. At the end of the novel, Maurice recognizes Clive's inconsistency and points it out to him:

I can't hang all my life on a little bit. You don't. You hang yours on Anne. You don't worry whether your relation with her is platonic or not, you only know it's big enough to hang a life on.

[*M*, p. 245]

After Clive's change Maurice suffers severe loneliness, a loneliness Forster portrays more successfully than any other emotion in the novel: "One cannot write those words too often: Maurice's loneliness: it increased" (*M*, p. 141). He has no one to talk to about his problems, a peculiar aspect of the homosexual plight that is not shared by heterosexual women: Margaret and Helen Schlegel can talk to each other. Maurice considers suicide but decides against it

when, in Forster's image, he is rejected by a female Death
(*M*, p. 139).

Maurice is horrified at his sexual awakening and refers
pejoratively to his physical attraction to Dickie as "Lust"
(*M*, p. 150). He feels that he has "cracked hideously" (*M*, p.
151). Because of Clive's influence, he does not yet realize
that being a sexual entity is not a hideous crack, and he
seeks aid from a doctor. Maurice equates lust with "sin" (*M*,
p. 155) and wants the doctor to punish him; his chief com-
plaint is pathetic: "I'm an unspeakable of the Oscar Wilde
sort" (*M*, p. 159). The awful judgment comes in the voice of
Dr. Barry: "Rubbish, rubbish!" (*M*, p. 159). Homosexuality
and decency seem incompatible to the good doctor, and he
knows Maurice "to be a decent fellow!" (*M*, p. 159), so he
refuses even to discuss Maurice's problem. Maurice is impressed: "was not Science speaking?" (*M*, p. 159).[16]

Maurice takes the doctor's advice and attempts to live a
heterosexual life. He does indeed want to marry, but for
the wrong, purely external reasons: he wants peace with
"society and the law" (*M*, p. 161), and he wants children.
The most he hopes for sexually in a heterosexual relationship is "a woman who was sympathetic in other ways"
(*M*, p. 161). Risley and Tchaikovsky save him from what obviously would have been an unsatisfactory marriage, and
Tchaikovsky's "spiritual and musical resurrection" (*M*, p.
162) with his nephew foreshadows Maurice's homosexual
communion and resurrection with Alec.

At the Tchaikovsky concert, Risley gives Maurice the
name of a hypnotist, and Maurice makes one last effort to

16. Joseph P. Eckhardt's excellent but unfortunately not yet published article,
"Frightening the Horses: The Late Victorian Public Emergence of Homosexuality," 1972, discusses the writings of Richard Burton, Edward Carpenter, John
Addington Symonds, and Havelock Ellis, and the life of Oscar Wilde; and, p. 4,
provides essential background to the climate of public opinion at the time: "Homosexuality was not a matter fit for discussion, and if it was mentioned, the common
term for such practices was Sodomy, a word that carried with it dire connotations
of divine judgment and threats of fire and brimstone. The laws against Sodomy
and other homosexual practices were strict."

become "normal," but Forster strongly implies that
Maurice's homosexuality is intrinsic and deep: "If this new
doctor could alter his being, was it not his duty to go,
though body and soul would be violated?" (*M,* p. 170).
Maurice's visits to the hypnotist to change what he knows to
be his true nature parallel Margaret Schlegel's admission to
Henry that she has been "naughty." Both are attempts to go
along with society's arbitrary roles, attempts to act the way
society says one should act rather than the way one personally knows is right.

Maurice feels that he will never be free of Clive "until
something greater intervened" (*M,* p. 170), and that something is physical homosexual love, not hypnotism and hypocritical heterosexuality. Going to the hypnotist is a regres-
sive act in which Maurice tries to recapture the trance of
childhood, when he was confused and bewildered; he is trying to escape self-knowledge. He has some brief success on
his first visit (*M,* p. 182), but after he meets Alec, he is no
longer susceptible; although his conscious desire to be
cured increases (*M,* p. 209), his unconscious desires prevent
him from going into a trance.

When the hypnotist gives up and tells Maurice to go
somewhere where homosexuality is legal, Maurice is surprised to hear that such places exist. Significantly, he is already using Alec's terminology: "You mean that a French-
man could share with a friend and yet not go to prison?"
(*M,* p. 211). The hypnotist doubts that the law will ever be
changed in England, for "England has always been disin-
clined to accept human nature" (*M,* p. 211); but Maurice
himself has done so: "He smiled sadly. 'It comes to this
then: there always have been people like me and always will
be, and generally they have been persecuted' " (*M,* p. 211).

Ironically, Clive's marriage directly effects Maurice's transcendent physical homosexuality: "Scudder was an importa-
tion—part of the larger life that had come into Penge with
politics and Anne" (*M,* p. 185). Anne functions as a Char-

lotte Bartlett character: she seemingly encourages Maurice's entrance into the armies of the benighted, in this novel hypocritical heterosexuality, but really works toward his acceptance of physical sexuality and Alec. Anne is frigid and a perfect match for Clive: when Maurice is upset after the cricket match, she immediately offers him ice (*M*, p. 203). Yet in spite of her frigidity, she keeps alive Maurice's consciousness of Alec by her questions about his lover's "bright brown eyes" (*M*, p. 184).

Maurice's two separate visits to Penge are symbolized by two kisses. On the first visit, when Maurice and Clive are in love, Clive refuses Maurice's kiss, setting the platonic pattern for their relationship (*M*, p. 93). On Maurice's last visit (actually his next-to-last), Clive kisses Maurice on the hand, and Maurice shudders (*M*, p. 175), as Miss Olcott had with him. Maurice's response is inspired: he "applied his lips to the starched cuff of a dress shirt" (*M*, p. 176), and their relationship is over.

He now cared less for Clive than Clive for him. That kiss had disillusioned. It was such a trivial prudish kiss, and alas! so typical. The less you had the more it was supposed to be—that was Clive's teaching.

[*M*, p. 184]

When Clive leaves the room after the kiss, Maurice calls "Come!" (*M*, p. 176) out the window for the first time; he has finally outgrown Clive's absurd antisexuality and is ready for Alec.

Clive's antisexuality is linked to his class snobbery. Clive cannot see servants as people and remarks about Alec, "You can't expect our standard of honesty in servants, any more than you can expect loyalty or gratitude" (*M*, p. 205). Forster's irony is staggering, for Alec is much more loyal to Maurice than is Clive. Before Alec, Maurice is as much a snob as Clive and tells Anne that the poor "haven't our feelings. They don't suffer as we should in their place" (*M*, pp.

167–68). Alec teaches Maurice the falsity of that remark, for he suffers from Maurice's rejection precisely as Maurice suffered from Clive's. Alec saves Maurice from Clive's negative influence in two ways, on both sex and class.

After Maurice "shares" with Alec for the first time, he loses his snobbery temporarily and tells Alec not to call him "sir" (*M*, p. 195). Their relationship exists on two levels: between Mr. Hall and Scudder; and between Maurice and Alec. It takes Maurice the last part of the novel to reach the personal from the social, and the trip is not easy for him. After he has sexual intercourse with Alec, he begins to develop a social conscience; his dream about his grandfather reveals something we did not know, that "he treated his own employees badly" (*M*, p. 197), something it would not have occurred to the old Maurice to mention. Even the awful device of jumping into windows functions as a symbol of class: Alec must climb a ladder to reach Maurice's window, but Maurice jumps directly into Clive's.

The cricket game further unites Maurice and Alec and connects with the night that precedes it (*M*, p. 201), a connection Clive and Anne never feel about their own sexual relationship. But Clive's appearance brings class into the cricket match (*M*, p. 201), and Maurice suspects Alec of "impertinence" (*M*, p. 202). Maurice feels himself a class traitor (*M*, p. 206), but his body saves him, in the tradition of Mr. Emerson: "his body would not be convinced. Chance had mated it too perfectly" (*M*, p. 207).

Alec's letter expresses his awareness of the difference in their classes: it begins, "Mr. Maurice. Dear Sir" (*M*, p. 207). "Dear Sir" defines the incongruous juxtaposition of their relationship, for Maurice is dear to Alec, but he is also "sir." The postscript to the letter achieves the purely personal; in his real concern that Maurice may be ill, Alec uses his first name for the only time (*M*, p. 207).

Maurice's feeling that he is a class traitor distorts his judgment so that he totally misreads Alec's actually very sweet letter. Maurice pounces on the sentence, "I have the key" (*M*, p. 208) and uses it as the key to his misinterpretation. The first meaning is straightforward: Alec has the key to the boathouse; the second meaning is less so. Although Maurice reads it as the key to blackmail, it actually refers to the key to love and happiness and picks up an image that recurs throughout the novel. When Maurice and Clive have their row about Ada, it ends with a key: "They touched with hostility, then parted for ever, the key falling between them" (*M*, p. 129). Clive has locked the door to protect Ada, thereby hurting Maurice, and he deserts Maurice for her: "Since Ada was in the passage Clive went out to her: to Woman was his first duty" (*M*, p. 130). When he leaves, Maurice locks the door between them, locking himself in loneliness and Clive out in the world with women (*M*, p. 130). Later, when Maurice waits up for Dickie, Dickie rejects his advances by announcing that he had a key, that Maurice's wait was futile (*M*, p. 148). *Maurice* is dedicated "To a Happier Year," and Forster asserts in the terminal note that "Happiness is its keynote" (*M*, p. 250). By misreading Alec's key to the boathouse, the first homosexual key to happiness in the novel, Maurice almost dooms himself to a life of loneliness.

By the time Maurice gets Alec's second letter, his class loyalties are breaking down; and he suggests to his family that "servants might be flesh and blood like ourselves" (*M*, p. 215). This admission implies an acceptance of the physical, of the "flesh," for the first time. Maurice shows real development and, also for the first time, can despise the hypocrisy of his "middle-middle" class clients (*M*, p. 218). In the British Museum he finally rejects both his class and Mr. Ducie's sexuality when he says his name is Scudder (*M*, p. 223).

When Maurice accepts Alec, Alec accepts Maurice. His blackmail attempt has been half-hearted at best and is merely the result of Maurice's having hurt his feelings. The

very fact that blackmail exists as a constant threat under-
scores the homosexual's position as outlaw in society:
Maurice himself was tempted to use it on Clive when his
own feelings were hurt by Clive's rejection (*M*, p. 135). Alec
is as confused as Maurice about the difference in their
classes: "gentlemen he knew, mates he knew; what class of
creature was Mr. Hall who said, 'Call me Maurice'?" (*M*, p.
220).

After their mutual acceptance in the British Museum,
Maurice can finally see clearly that both he and Alec have
been driven by fear: he of blackmail, Alec of him (*M*, p.
226). Maurice realizes that he did not meet Alec at the boathouse because of "muddle" (*M*, p. 226); he has been muddled throughout the novel, but now for the first time he
knows it, and he knows it about both sex and class. He realizes that although he has been pretending that Alec is evil,
what in fact is evil is the "situation" (*M*, p. 226) in which all
homosexuals find themselves.

When Maurice and Alec spend their second night
together, Alec tells Maurice of his resentment of the upper
class's attitude toward servants, and he expresses his resentment physically (*M*, p. 229). He is no longer deferential
(*M*, p. 228), and their relationship is finally both passionate
and equal. When Alec chooses to miss his boat, Maurice's
vision of their future life in the greenwood finally overcomes class barriers:

They must live outside class, without relations or money; they
must work and stick to each other till death. But England belonged to them. That, besides companionship, was their reward.
Her air and sky were theirs, not the timorous millions' who own
stuffy little boxes, but never their own souls.

[*M*, p. 239]

In the terminal note, Forster succinctly describes Alec's
development: "from the masculine blur past which Maurice
drives into Penge, through the croucher beside the piano

and the rejecter of a tip and the haunter of shrubberies and the stealer of apricots into the sharer who gives and takes love" (*M*, p. 253). Alec is always identified with nature, like Stephen Wonham in *The Longest Journey,* but Maurice is more sensitive to Alec than Rickie is to Stephen: "as he touched the carapace of his dress shirt a sense of ignominy came over him, and he felt he had no right to criticise anyone who lived in the open air" (*M*, p. 185). When Maurice bumps into Alec in the garden, Alec is "escaping from Mr. Borenius" (*M*, p. 187); he escapes from marriage and conventional Christianity to Maurice and physical homosexual communion, for Maurice has just partaken of and been "heated" by "Food and wine" (*M*, p. 187).

When Maurice bumps into Alec, he connects all the previously unconnected events and realizes that "he had been alive" (*M*, p. 188), but he is not yet ready to accept that knowledge, and the image of darkness recurs: "when he reached 'now', it was as if an electric current passed through the chain of insignificant events so that he dropped it and let it smash back into darkness" (*M*, p. 188). When he reenters the house, his hair is "all yellow with evening primrose pollen" (*M*, p. 188), and Mrs. Durham calls him "bacchanalian" (*M*, p. 188).

Forster wrote that as he worked on him, Alec "became less of a comrade and more of a person" (*M*, p. 252). Alec is indeed a person, and he exhibits sensitivity and insight when he notices that Maurice looks at him "angry and gentle both together" (*M*, p. 195) the first time he sees him. Maurice's reentry into society after the first time they sleep together is described as a descent (*M*, p. 199), for their love is above it.

After Maurice has been written off by science, he becomes more human and finds it easier to accept Alec as human (*M*, p. 215). He realizes that Alec is like himself in many ways, and he does not make Clive's mistake about *The Symposium* when he reads Alec's second letter:

He didn't want such a letter, he didn't know what it wanted—half a dozen things possibly—but he couldn't well be cold and hard over it as Clive had been to him over the original *Symposium* business, and argue, "Here's a certain statement, I shall keep you to it."

[*M*, p. 217]

In the British Museum, Maurice is human and mischievous and talks about the weather, telling Alec that there have been "two fine days. And one fine night" (*M*, p. 220). Although Alec is trying to blackmail him, Maurice looks for his motives: "Maurice found himself trying to get underneath the words" (*M*, p. 221). Their eyes meet and they smile, fittingly, at the statue of a "winged Assyrian bull" with five legs (*M*, p. 222). When Alec asks Maurice to spend the night with him, Maurice answers that he has an engagement (*M*, p. 227), but he breaks it and goes with Alec; in Ansell's terms, Maurice is engaged to Alec, and nothing else matters. When they meet at "Boathouse, Penge" (*M*, p. 239), they have their last reunion, for they have communicated without words and have achieved permanent communion: "And now we shan't be parted no more, and that's finished" (*M*, p. 240).

All that remains is for Maurice to say goodbye to Clive, who he finally realizes belongs "to the past" (*M*, p. 245)—personally, in his love affair with Maurice; socially, in his snobbish class values; and emotionally, in his sexual intolerance. When Clive hears that Alec has missed his boat, his comment expresses a class condescension that Maurice has rejected: "These people are impossible" (*M*, p. 244). Clive is equally reactionary in his attitude toward the freedom of women and regrets Maurice's homosexuality because "he had assumed Maurice was normal during the last fortnight, and so encouraged Anne's intimacy" (*M*, p. 242); presumably otherwise he would have "protected" her from one more aspect of life.

Clive is upset to hear that Maurice is still homosexual,

and his imagery is striking: "You gave me to understand that the land through the looking-glass was behind you at last" (*M*, pp. 242–43). Maurice's goal throughout the novel has been to accept the looking-glass he feared as a child, and Clive's negative image assures us that he has finally done so. Maurice tells Clive that he has slept with Alec in "the Russet Room" (*M*, p. 244), and the two relationships are contrasted by color: Maurice's cool, platonic affair with Clive in the Blue Room (*M*, p. 203) is finally superseded by a more complete, hot, passionate, and physical love in the Red.

Clive is shocked by Maurice's announcements and cannot realize that "he and Maurice were alike descended from the Clive of two years ago, the one by respectability, the other by rebellion" (*M*, p. 245), nor that they would go on becoming more and more different. Maurice, who has accepted that difference, disappears as Clive is talking and leaves "no trace of his presence except a little pile of the petals of the evening primrose, which mourned from the ground like an expiring fire" (*M*, p. 246). Earlier, Maurice has had to discover for himself the odor of those flowers; "Clive had shown him evening primroses in the past, but had never told him they smelt" (*M*, pp. 184–85). Clive omits the sensual aspect, but Maurice learns it in the garden, the night he first shares with Alec, and he affirms it at the end of the novel by going off to live in the greenwood. Clive never knows for certain when Maurice leaves, and the novel ends with a negative vision of conventional society, with Clive going indoors "to devise some method of concealing the truth from Anne" (*M*, p. 246). To the last, the benighted, seeing their duty to be the concealment of truth, conceal from themselves life, imtimate connection, and the possibility of uniqueness.

Bibliography

WORKS OF E. M. FORSTER

Abinger Harvest. New York, Harcourt, Brace, 1936.

Albergo Empedocle and Other Writings. Edited by George H. Thomson. New York, Liveright, 1971.

Alexandria: A History and a Guide [1922]. Garden City, N.Y., Doubleday, Anchor, 1961.

Aspects of the Novel [1927]. Reprint, New York, Harcourt, Brace and World, Harvest, 1956.

The Celestial Omnibus and Other Stories [1911]. New York, Knopf, 1923.

England's Pleasant Land: A Pageant Play. London, Hogarth, 1940.

The Eternal Moment and Other Stories. New York, Harcourt, Brace, 1928.

Goldsworthy Lowes Dickinson. New York, Harcourt, Brace, 1934.

The Hill of Devi. New York, Harcourt Brace Jovanovich, Harvest, 1953.

Howards End [1910]. New York, Knopf, 1946; reprint, New York, Random House, Vintage, 1954.

The Life to Come and Other Stories. New York, Norton, 1972.

The Longest Journey [1907]. New York, Knopf, 1953; reprint, New York, Random House, Vintage, n.d.

Marianne Thornton: A Domestic Biography 1797–1887. New York, Harcourt, Brace, 1956.

Maurice. New York, Norton, 1971; reprint, New York, Signet, 1973.

A Passage to India. New York, Harcourt, Brace, 1924; reprint, New York, Harcourt, Brace and World, Harvest, 1965.

Pharos and Pharillon. 2d ed. Richmond, Surrey, Hogarth, 1923.

A Room with a View [1908]. New York, Knopf, 1953; reprint, New York, Random House, Vintage, 1961.

Two Cheers for Democracy. New York, Harcourt, Brace, 1938.

"A View Without a Room: Old Friends Fifty Years Later." *New York Times Book Review,* July 27, 1958, p. 4.

Where Angels Fear to Tread [1905]. New York, Knopf, 1950; reprint, New York, Random House, Vintage, 1958.

CRITICAL WORKS AND COMMENTARY

Ackerley, J. R. *My Father and Myself.* New York, Coward-McCann, 1969.

Alvarez, A. "E. M. Forster: From Snobbery to Love." *Saturday Review,* October 16, 1971, pp. 39–43.

Annan, Noel. "Love Story." *New York Review of Books,* October 21, 1971, pp. 12–19.

Austin, Don. "The Problem of Continuity in Three Novels of E. M. Forster." *Modern Fiction Studies,* 2 (Autumn 1961), 217–29.

Barger, Evert. "Memories of Morgan." *New York Times Book Review,* August 16, 1970, pp. 2; 32–35.

Beer, J. B. *The Achievement of E. M. Forster.* New York, Barnes and Noble, 1962.

Bell, Quentin. *Virginia Woolf: A Biography.* New York, Harcourt Brace Jovanovich, 1972.

Bradbury, Malcolm, ed. *Forster: A Collection of Critical Essays.* Englewood Cliffs, N.J., Prentice-Hall, 1966.

Brander, Laurence. *E. M. Forster: A Critical Study.* London, Hart-Davis, 1968.

Brown, E. K. *Rhythm in the Novel.* Toronto, University of Toronto Press, 1950.

Carpenter, Edward. *Homogenic Love, and Its Place in a Free Society.* Manchester, England, The Labour Press Society Limited, 1894 (printed for private circulation only).

"A Chalice for Youth." *Times Literary Supplement,* October 8, 1971, pp. 1215–16.

Crews, Frederick C. *E. M. Forster: The Perils of Humanism.* Princeton, Princeton University Press, 1962.

Eckhardt, Joseph P. "Frightening the Horses: The Late Victorian Public Emergence of Homosexuality." Unpublished essay, 1972.

Edgerton, Patricia. "The Androgynous Mind: Consideration of E. M. Forster and Virginia Woolf." Unpublished M.A. thesis, Columbia University, 1956.

Epstein, Joseph. *"Maurice."* *New York Times Book Review,* October 10, 1971, pp. 1–2, 24–29.

Furbank, P. N. "The Personality of E. M. Forster." *Encounter,* October 11, 1970, pp. 61–68.

——, and F. J. H. Haskell. "Interview with E. M. Forster." *Paris Review,* 1–4 (Spring 1953), 29–41.

Godfrey, Denis. *E. M. Forster's Other Kingdom.* Edinburgh and London, Oliver and Boyd, 1968.

Gransden, K. W. *E. M. Forster.* Edinburgh and London, Oliver and Boyd, 1962.

Hall, James. *The Tragic Comedians; Seven Modern British Novelists.* Bloomington, Indiana University Press, 1963.

Heilbrun, Carolyn G. "The Bloomsbury Group." *Midway,* Autumn 1968, pp. 71–85.

——. *Toward a Recognition of Androgyny.* New York, Knopf, 1973.

——. "The Woman as Hero." *Texas Quarterly,* 8 (Winter 1965), 132–41.

Holroyd, Michael. *Lytton Strachey: A Critical Biography.* London, Heinemann, 1967.

Howarth, Herbert. Lectures, University of Pennsylvania. November 1, 8, 15, and 22, 1967.

Hynes, Samuel. *The Edwardian Turn of Mind.* Princeton, Princeton University Press, 1968.

Johnstone, J. K. *The Bloomsbury Group: A Study of E. M. Forster, Lytton Strachey, Virginia Woolf, and their Circle.* New York, Noonday Press, 1954.

Jones, David. "E. M. Forster on His Life and His Books." *Listener,* 61 (January 1, 1959), 11–12.

Kelvin, Norman. *E. M. Forster.* Carbondale and Edwardsville, Southern Illinois University Press, 1967.

Kermode, Frank. "A Queer Business." *Atlantic Monthly,* November 1, 1971, pp. 140–44.

Kirkpatrick, B. J. *A Bibliography of E. M. Forster.* London, Hart–Davis, 1968.

Lehmann-Haupt, Christopher. "A Major 'New' Forster Novel." *New York Times,* October 1, 1971, p. 39.

Lester, John A. *Journey through Despair 1880–1914: Transformations in British Literary Culture.* Princeton, Princeton University Press, 1968.

Levine, June Perry. *Creation and Criticism:* A Passage to India. Lincoln, University of Nebraska Press, 1971.

Macaulay, Rose. *The Writings of E. M. Forster.* New York, Harcourt, Brace, 1938.

McConkey, James. *The Novels of E. M. Forster.* Ithaca, N.Y., Cornell University Press, 1957.

McDowell, Frederick P. W. *E. M. Forster.* New York, Twayne, 1969.

——. "E. M. Forster: An Annotated Secondary Bibliography." *English Literature in Transition,* 13 (1970), 93–173.

——. "The E. M. Forster Bibliography of Secondary Writings: Some Preliminary Observations." *English Literature in Transition,* 13 (1970), 89–92.

Martin, Kingsley. *Father Figures: A First Volume of Autobiography 1897–1931.* London, Hutchinson, 1966.

Mintz, Alan. "Varieties of Homosexual Society and the Early Novels of Forster." Unpublished essay, 1969.

Moody, Phillipa. *A Critical Commentary on E. M. Forster's* A Passage to India. New York, St. Martin's, 1968.

Moore, Harry T. *E. M. Forster.* New York, Columbia University Press, 1965.

Mosely, Edwin A. "A New Correlative for *Howards End:* Demeter and Persephone." *Lock Haven Bulletin,* Series 1, No. 3 (1961), pp. 1–6.

Oliver, H. J. *The Art of E. M. Forster*. Melbourne, Australia, Melbourne University Press, 1960.

Ozick, Cynthia. "Forster as Homosexual." *Commentary*, 52 (December 1971) 81–85.

Pittenger, Norman. "E. M. Forster, Homosexuality and Christian Morality." *Christian Century*, December 15, 1971, pp. 1468–71.

Plato. *The Symposium*. Trans. Walter Hamilton. Harmondsworth, Middlesex, Penguin, 1951.

Pritchett, V. S. "The Upholstered Prison." *New Statesman*, October 8, 1971, pp. 478–80.

Rose, Martial. *E. M. Forster*. London, Evans Brothers, 1970.

Rosenthal, M. L. "Only Connect." *Spectator*, 217 (September 23, 1966), 383–84.

Rutherford, Andrew, ed. *Twentieth Century Interpretations of* A Passage to India: *A Collection of Critical Essays*. Englewood Cliffs, N.J., Prentice-Hall, 1970.

Saunders, Charles Richard. *Lytton Strachey: His Mind and Art*. New Haven, Yale University Press, 1957.

Shahane, V. A., ed. *Perspectives on E. M. Forster's* A Passage to India: *A Collection of Critical Essays*. New York, Barnes and Noble, 1968.

Shaw, George Bernard. *Man and Superman: A Comedy and a Philosophy*. New York, Brentano's, 1905; Baltimore, Md., Penguin, 1952, reprint, 1962.

Spender, Stephen. "Forster's Queer Novel." *Partisan Review*, No. 1 (1972), 113–17.

Stallybrass, Oliver, ed. *Aspects of E. M. Forster: Essays and Recollections Written for His Ninetieth Birthday January 1, 1969*. New York, Harcourt, Brace and World, 1969.

Steiner, George. "Under the Greenwood Tree." *New Yorker*, October 9, 1971, pp. 158–69.

Stone, Wilfred. *The Cave and the Mountain: A Study of E. M. Forster*. Stanford, Stanford University Press, 1966.

Taylor, Rachel Annand. "The Post-War English Novel." *Sociological Review*, 20 (July 1928), 177–96.

Thomson, George H. *The Fiction of E. M. Forster*. Detroit, Wayne State University Press, 1967.

Thomson, George H. "The Perils of E. M. Forster's Critics." *Dalhousie Review,* 42 (Winter 1962–63), 492–98.

Tindall, William York. *A Reader's Guide to James Joyce.* New York, Noonday-Farrar, Straus and Giroux, 1959.

Trilling, Diana. "The Uncomplaining Homosexuals." *Harper's,* August 1969, pp. 90–95.

Trilling, Lionel. *E. M. Forster.* Norfolk, Conn., New Directions, 1943.

Tuohy, Frank. "The English Question." *Spectator,* 209 (July 6, 1962), 30–31.

Wescott, Glenway. "A Dinner, A Talk, A Walk with Forster." *New York Times Book Review,* October 10, 1971, pp. 2; 18–22.

Wilde, Alan. *Art and Order: A Study of E. M. Forster.* New York, New York University Press, 1964.

Wilson, Angus. "A Conversation with E. M. Forster." *Encounter,* 9 (1957), 52–57.

Index